John Henry Newman

**A Letter to the Rev. E.B. Pusey, D.D. on his Recent Eirenicon**

John Henry Newman

**A Letter to the Rev. E.B. Pusey, D.D. on his Recent Eirenicon**

ISBN/EAN: 9783744689045

Printed in Europe, USA, Canada, Australia, Japan

Cover: Foto ©Lupo / pixelio.de

More available books at **www.hansebooks.com**

# A LETTER

LONDON:
GILBERT AND RIVINGTON, PRINTERS,
ST. JOHN'S SQUARE.

# A LETTER,

*&c.*

No one who desires the union of Christendom after its many and long-standing divisions, can have any other feeling than joy, my dear Pusey, at finding from your recent Volume, that you see your way to make definite proposals to us for effecting that great object, and are able to lay down the basis and conditions on which you could co-operate in advancing it. It is not necessary that we should concur in the details of your scheme, or in the principles which it involves, in order to welcome the important fact, that, with your personal knowledge of the Anglican body, and your experience of its composition and tendencies, you consider the time to be come when you and your friends may, without imprudence, turn your minds to the contemplation of such an enterprise. Even were you an individual member of that Church, a watchman upon a high tower in a metropolis of religious opinion, we should naturally listen with interest to what you had to report of the state of the sky and the progress of the night, what stars were mounting up or what clouds gathering,—what were the prospects of the three great parties which Anglicanism contains within it, and what was just now the action upon them respectively of the politics and science of the time. You do not go into these matters; but the step you have taken is evidently the measure and the issue of the view which you have formed of them all.

However, you are not a mere individual; from early youth you have devoted yourself to the Established Church, and, after between forty and fifty years of unremitting labour in its service, your roots and your branches stretch out through every portion of its large territory. You, more than any one else alive, have been the present and untiring agent by whom a great work has been effected in it; and, far more than is usual, you have received in your life-time, as well as merited, the confidence of your brethren. You cannot speak merely for yourself; your antecedents, your existing influence, are a pledge to us, that what you may determine will be the determination of a multitude. Numbers, too, for whom you cannot properly be said to speak, will be moved by your authority or your arguments; and numbers, again, who are of a school more recent than your own, and who are only not your followers because they have outstripped you in their free speeches and demonstrative acts in our behalf, will, for the occasion, accept you as their spokesman. There is no one any where,—among ourselves, in your own body, or, I suppose, in the Greek Church,—who can affect so large a circle of men, so virtuous, so able, so learned, so zealous, as come, more or less, under your influence; and I cannot pay them a greater compliment, than to tell them they ought all to be Catholics, nor do them a more affectionate service than to pray that they may one day become such. Nor can I address myself to an act more pleasing, as I trust, to the Divine Lord of the Church, or more loyal and dutiful to His Vicar on earth, than to attempt, however feebly, to promote so great a consummation.

I know the joy it would give those conscientious men, of whom I am speaking, to be one with ourselves. I know how their hearts spring up with a spontaneous transport at the very thought of union; and what yearning is theirs after that great privilege, which they have not, communion with the see of Peter, and its present, past, and future. I conjecture it by what I used to feel myself, while yet in the Anglican Church. I recollect well what an outcast I seemed to myself, when I took down from the shelves of my library the volumes of St. Athanasius or St. Basil, and set myself to study them; and how, on the contrary, when at length I was brought into Catholic Communion, I kissed them with delight, with a feeling that in them I had more than all that I had lost, and, as though I were directly addressing the glorious saints, who bequeathed them to the Church, I said to the inanimate pages, "You are now mine, and I am now yours, beyond any mistake." Such, I conceive, would be the joy of the persons I speak of, if they could wake up one morning, and find themselves rightfully possessed of Catholic traditions and hopes, without violence to their own sense of duty;—and, certainly, I am the last man to say that such violence is in any case lawful, that the claims of conscience are not paramount, or that any one may overleap what he deliberately holds to be God's command, in order to make his path easier for him or his heart lighter.

I am the last man to quarrel with this jealous deference to the voice of our conscience, whatever judgment others may form of us in consequence, for this reason,—because their case, as it at present stands, has, as you know, been my own. You recollect well what hard things were said against us twenty-five years ago, which we knew in our hearts we did not deserve. Hence, I am now in the position of the fugitive Queen in the well-known passage; who, "haud ignara mali" herself, had learned to sympathize with those who were the inheritors of her past wanderings. There were Priests, good men, whose zeal outstripped their knowledge, and who in consequence spoke confidently, when they would have been wiser, had they suspended their adverse judgment of those whom they had soon to welcome as brethren in communion. We at that time were in worse plight than your friends are now, for our opponents put their very hardest thoughts of us into print. One of them wrote thus in a Letter addressed to one of the Catholic Bishops:—

"That this Oxford crisis is a real progress to Catholicism, I have all along considered a perfect delusion. . . . I look upon Mr. Newman, Dr. Pusey, and their associates, as wily and crafty, though unskilful guides. . . . The embrace of Mr. Newman is the kiss that would betray us. . . . But,— what is the most striking feature in the rancorous malignity of these men,—their calumnies are often lavished upon us, when we should be led to think that the subject-matter of their treatises closed every avenue against their vituperation. The three last volumes [of the Tracts] have opened my eyes to the craftiness and the cunning, as well as the malice, of the members of the Oxford Convention. . . . If the Puseyites are to be the new Apostles of Great Britain, my hopes for my country are lowering and gloomy. . . . I would never have consented to enter the lists against this strange confraternity. . . . if I did not feel that my own Prelate was opposed to the guile and treachery of these men. . . . I impeach Dr. Pusey and his friends of a deadly hatred of our religion. . . . What, my Lord, would the Holy See think of the works of these Puseyites? . . ."

Another priest, himself a convert, wrote:—

"As we approach towards Catholicity, our love and respect increases, and our violence dies away; but the bulk of these men become more rabid as they become like Rome, a plain proof of their designs. . . . I do not believe that they are any nearer the portals of the Catholic Church than the most prejudiced Methodist and Evangelical preacher. . . . Such, Rev. Sir, is an outline of my views on the Oxford movement."

I do not say that such a view of us was unnatural; and, for myself, I readily confess, that I had used about the Church such language, that I had no claim on Catholics for any mercy. But, after all, and in fact, they were wrong in their anticipations,—nor did their brethren agree with them at the time. Especially Dr. Wiseman (as he was then) took a larger and more generous view of us; nor did the Holy See interfere, though the writer of one of these passages invoked its judgment. The event showed that the more cautious line of conduct was the more prudent; and one of the Bishops, who had taken part against us, with a supererogation of charity, sent me on his deathbed an expression of his sorrow for having in past years mistrusted me. A faulty conscience, faithfully obeyed, through God's mercy, had in the long run brought me right.

Fully, then, do I recognize the rights of conscience in this matter. I find no fault with your stating, as clearly and completely as you can, the difficulties which stand in the way of your joining us. I cannot wonder that you begin with stipulating conditions of union, though I do not concur in them myself, and think that in the event you yourself would be content to let them drop. Such representations as yours are necessary to open the subject in debate; they ascertain how the land lies, and serve to clear the ground. Thus I begin: —but after allowing as much as this, I am obliged in honesty to say what I fear, my dear Pusey, will pain you. Yet I am confident, my very dear Friend, that at least you will not be angry with me if I say, what I must say, or say nothing at all, that there is much both in the matter and in the manner of your Volume, calculated to wound those who love you well, but love truth more. So it is; with the best motives and kindest intentions,— " Cædimur, et totidem plagis consumimus hostem." We give you a sharp cut, and you return it. You complain of our being "dry, hard, and unsympathizing;" and we answer that you are unfair and irritating. But we at least have not professed to be composing an Irenicon, when we treated you as foes. There was one of old time who wreathed his sword in myrtle; excuse me— you discharge your olive-branch as if from a catapult.

Do not think I am not serious; if I spoke seriously, I should seem to speak harshly. Who will venture to assert, that the hundred pages which you have devoted to the Blessed Virgin give other than a one-sided view of our teaching about her, little suited to win us? It may be a salutary castigation, if any of us have fairly provoked it, but it is not making the best of matters; it is not smoothing the way for an understanding or a compromise. It leads a writer in the most moderate and liberal Anglican newspaper of the day, the "Guardian," to turn away from your representation of us with horror. " It is language," says your Reviewer, " which, after having often heard it, we still can only hear with horror. We had rather not quote any of it, or of the comments upon it." What could an Exeter Hall orator, what could a Scotch commentator on the Apocalypse, do more for his own side of the controversy in the picture he drew of us? You may be sure that what creates horror on one side, will be answered by indignation on the other, and these are not the most favourable dispositions for a peace conference. I had been accustomed to think, that you, who in times past were ever less declamatory in controversy than myself, now that years had gone on, and circumstances changed, had come to look on our old warfare against Rome as cruel and inexpedient. Indeed, I know that it was a chief objection urged against me only last year by persons who agreed with you in deprecating an Oratory at Oxford, which at that time was in prospect, that such an undertaking would be the signal for the rekindling of that fierce style of polemics which is now out of date. I had fancied you shared in that opinion; but now, as if to show how imperative you deem its renewal, you actually bring to life one of my own strong sayings in 1841, which had long been in the grave,—that " the Roman Church comes as near to idolatry as can be supposed in a Church, of which it is said, ' The idols He shall utterly abolish.' "—p. 111.

## INTRODUCTION. 11

I know, indeed, and feel deeply, that your frequent references, in your Volume, to what I have lately or formerly written, are caused by your strong desire to be still one with me as far as you can, and by that true affection, which takes pleasure in dwelling on such sayings of mine as you can still accept with the full approbation of your judgment. I trust I am not ungrateful or irresponsive to you in this respect; but other considerations have an imperative claim to be taken into account. Pleasant as it is to agree with you, I am bound to explain myself in cases in which I have changed my mind, or have given a wrong impression of my meaning, or have been wrongly reported; and, while I trust that I have higher than such personal motives for addressing you in print, yet it will serve to introduce my main subject, and give me an opportunity for remarks which bear upon it indirectly, if I dwell for a page or two on such matters contained in your Volume as concern myself.

1. The mistake which I have principally in view is the belief which is widely spread, that I have publicly spoken of the Anglican Church as "the great bulwark against infidelity in this land." In a pamphlet of yours a year old, you spoke of "a very earnest body of Roman Catholics," who "rejoice in all the workings of God the Holy Ghost in the Church of England (whatever they think of her), and are saddened by what weakens her who

is, in God's hands, the great bulwark against infidelity in this land." The concluding words you were thought to quote from my *Apologia*. In consequence, Dr. Manning, now our Archbishop, replied to you, asserting, as you say, " the contradictory of that statement." In that counter-assertion, he was at the time generally considered (rightly or wrongly as it may be), though writing to you, to be really correcting statements in my *Apologia*, without introducing my name. Further, in the Volume, which you have now published, you recur to the saying; and you speak of its author in terms, which, did I not know your partial kindness for me, would hinder me from identifying him with myself. You say, " The saying was not mine, but that of one of the deepest thinkers and observers in the Roman Communion," p. 7. A friend has suggested to me that perhaps you mean De Maistre; and, from an anonymous letter which I have received from Dublin, I find it is certain that the very words in question were once used by Archbishop Murray; but you speak of the author of them as if now alive. At length, a reviewer of your Volume in the " Weekly Register," distinctly attributes them to me by name, and gives me the first opportunity I have had of disowning them; and this I now do. What, at some time or other, I may have said in conversation or private letter, of course, I cannot tell; but I have never, I am sure, used the word "bulwark" of the Anglican Church deliberately. What I said in my *Apologia* was this:—That that Church was "a serviceable breakwater against errors more fundamental than its own." A bulwark is an integral part of the thing it defends; whereas the words "serviceable" and "breakwater" imply a kind of protection, which is accidental and *de facto*. Again, in saying that the Anglican Church is a defence against "errors more fundamental than its own," I imply that it has errors, and those fundamental.

2. There is another passage in your Volume, at p. 337, which it may be right to observe upon. You have made a collection of passages from the Fathers, as witnesses in behalf of your doctrine that the whole Christian faith is contained in Scripture, as if, in your sense of the words, Catholics contradicted you here. And you refer to my Notes on St. Athanasius as contributing passages to your list; but, after all, neither do you, nor do I in my Notes, affirm any doctrine which Rome denies. Those Notes also make frequent reference to a traditional teaching, which (be the faith ever so certainly contained in Scripture), still is necessary as a Regula Fidei, for showing us that it is contained there; vid. pp. 283, 344; and this tradition, I know, you uphold as fully as I do in the Notes in question. In consequence, you allow that there is a twofold rule, Scripture and Tradition; and this is all that Catholics say. How, then, do Anglicans differ from Rome here? I believe the difference is merely one of words; and I shall be doing, so far, the work

of an Irenicon, if I make clear what this verbal difference is. Catholics and Anglicans (I do not say Protestants), attach different meanings to the word "proof," in the controversy whether the whole faith is, or is not, contained in Scripture. We mean that not every article of faith is so contained there, that it may thence be logically proved, *independently* of the teaching and authority of the Tradition; but Anglicans mean that every article of faith is so contained there, that it may thence be proved, *provided* there be added the illustrations and compensations supplied by the Tradition. And it is in this latter sense that the Fathers also speak in the passages which you quote from them. I am sure at least that St. Athanasius frequently adduces passages in proof of points in controversy, which no one would see to be proofs, unless Apostolical Tradition were taken into account, first as suggesting, then as authoritatively ruling their meaning. Thus, *you* do not deny, that the whole is not in Scripture in such sense that pure unaided logic can draw it from the sacred text; nor do *we* deny, that the faith is in Scripture, in an improper sense, in the sense that *Tradition* is able to recognize and determine it there. You do not profess to dispense with Tradition; nor do we forbid the idea of probable, secondary, symbolical, connotative, senses of Scripture, over and above those which properly belong to the wording and context. I hope you will agree with me in this.

3. Nor is it only in isolated passages that you give me a place in your Volume. A considerable portion of it is written with a reference to two publications of mine, one of which you name and defend, the other you implicitly protest against; Tract 90, and the Essay on Doctrinal Development. As to Tract 90, you have from the first, as all the world knows, boldly stood up for it, in spite of the obloquy which it brought upon you, and have done me a great service. You are now republishing it with my cordial concurrence; but I take this opportunity of noticing, lest there should be any mistake on the part of the public, that you do so with a different object from that which I had when I wrote it. Its original purpose was simply that of justifying myself and others in subscribing to the 39 Articles, while professing many tenets which had popularly been considered distinctive of the Roman faith. I considered that my interpretation of the Articles, as I gave it in that Tract, would stand, provided the parties imposing them allowed it; otherwise, I thought it could not stand: and, when in the event the Bishops and public opinion did not allow it, I gave up my Living, as having no right to retain it. My feeling about the interpretation is expressed in a passage in Loss and Gain, which runs thus:—

"'Is it,' asked Reding, 'a received view?' 'No view is received,' said the other; 'the Articles themselves are received, but there is no authoritative interpretation of them at all.' 'Well,' said Reding, 'is it a tolerated view?' 'It certainly has been strongly opposed,' answered Bateman; 'but it has never been condemned.' 'That is no answer,' said Charles. 'Does any one Bishop hold it? Did any one Bishop ever hold it? Has it ever been formally admitted as tenable by any one Bishop? Is it a view got up to meet existing difficulties, or has it an historical existence?' Bateman could give only one answer to these questions, as they were successively put to him. 'I thought so,' said Charles; 'the view is specious certainly. I don't see why it might not have done, had it been tolerably sanctioned; but you have no sanction to show me. As it stands, it is a mere theory struck out by individuals. Our Church *might* have adopted this mode of interpreting the Articles; but, from what you tell me, it certainly has not done so.' "—Ch. 15.

However, the Tract did not carry its object and conditions on its face, and necessarily lay open to interpretations very far from the true one. Dr. Wiseman (as he then was), in particular, with the keen apprehension which was his characteristic, at once saw in it a basis of accommodation between Anglicanism and Rome. He suggested broadly that the decrees of the Council of Trent should be made the rule of interpretation for the 39 Articles, a proceeding, of which Sancta Clara, I think, had set the example; and, as you have observed, published a letter to Lord Shrewsbury on the subject, of which the following are extracts:—

" We Catholics must necessarily deplore [England's] separation as a deep moral evil,—as a state of schism, of which nothing can justify the continuance. Many members of the Anglican Church view it in the same light as to the first point —its sad evil; though they excuse their individual position in it as an unavoidable misfortune. . . . We may depend upon a willing, an able, and a most zealous co-operation with any effort which we may make, towards bringing her into her rightful position, in Catholic unity with the Holy See and the Churches of its obedience,—in other words, with the Church Catholic. Is this a visionary idea? Is it merely the expression of a strong desire? I know that many will so judge it; and, perhaps, were I to consult my own quiet, I would not venture to express it. But I will, in simplicity of heart, cling to hopefulness, cheered, as I feel it, by so many promising appearances. . . .

"A natural question here presents itself;—what facilities appear in the present state of things for bringing about so happy a consummation, as the reunion of England to the Catholic Church, beyond what have before existed, and particularly under Archbishops Laud or Wake. It strikes me, many. First, &c. . . . A still more promising circumstance I think your Lordship will with me consider the *plan* which the eventful Tract No. 90 has pursued, and in which Mr. Ward, Mr. Oakeley, and even Dr. Pusey have agreed. I allude to the method of *bringing their doctrines into accordance with ours by explanation.* A foreign priest has pointed out to us a valuable document for our consideration,—' Bossuet's Reply to the Pope,'—when consulted on the best method of reconciling the followers of the Augsburg Confession with the Holy See. The learned Bishop observes, that Providence had allowed so much Catholic truth to be preserved in that Confession, that full advantage should be taken of the circumstance; that no retractations should be demanded, but an explanation of the Confession in accordance with Catholic doctrines. Now, for such a method as this, the way is in part prepared by the demonstration that such interpretation may be given of the most difficult Articles, as will strip them of all contradiction to the decrees of the Tridentine Synod. The same method may be pursued on other points; and much pain may thus be spared to individuals, and much difficulty to the Church."—Pp. 11. 35. 38.

This use of my Tract, so different from my own, but sanctioned by the great name of our Cardinal, you are now reviving; and I gather from your doing so, that your Bishops and the opinion of the public are likely now, or in prospect, to admit what twenty-five years ago they refused. On this point, much as it rejoices me to know your anticipation, of course, I cannot have an opinion.

4. So much for Tract 90. On the other hand, as to my hypothesis of Doctrinal Development, I am sorry to find you do not look upon it with friendly eyes; though how, without its aid, you can maintain the doctrines of the Holy Trinity and Incarnation, and others which you hold, I cannot understand. You consider my principle may be the means, in time to come, of introducing into our Creed, as portions of the necessary Catholic faith, the Infallibility of the Pope, and various opinions, pious or profane, as it may be, about our Blessed Lady. I hope to remove your anxiety as to these consequences, before I bring my observations to an end; at present I notice it as my apology for interfering in a controversy which at first sight is no business of mine.

5. I have another reason for writing; and that is, unless it is rude in me to say so, because you seem to think writing does not become me, as being a convert. I do not like silently to acquiesce in such a judgment. You say at p. 98:—

"Nothing can be more unpractical than for an individual to throw himself into the Roman Church, because he could accept the *letter* of the Council of Trent. Those who were born Roman Catholics, have a liberty, which, in the nature of things, a person could not have, who left another system, to embrace that of Rome. I cannot imagine how any faith could stand the shock of leaving one system, criticizing *it*, and cast himself into another system, criticizing *it*. For myself, I have always felt that had (which God of His mercy avert hereafter also) the English Church, by accepting heresy, driven me out of it, I could have gone in no other way than that of closing my eyes, and accepting whatever was put before me. But a liberty which individuals could not use, and explanations, which, so long as they remain individual, must be unauthoritative, might be formally made by the Church of Rome to the Church of England as the basis of re-union."

And again, p. 210 :—

" It seems to me to be a psychological impossibility for one who has already exchanged one system for another to make those distinctions. One who, by his own act, places himself under authority, cannot make conditions about his submission. But definite explanations of our Articles have, before now, been at least tentatively offered to us, on the Roman and Greek side, as sufficient to restore communion; and the Roman explanations too were, in most cases, mere supplements to our Articles, on points upon which our Church had not spoken."

Now passages such as these seem almost a challenge to me to speak; and to keep silence would be to assent to the justice of them. At the cost, then, of speaking about myself, of which I feel there has been too much of late, I observe upon them as follows:—Of course, as you say, a convert comes to learn, and not to pick and choose. He comes in simplicity and confidence, and it does not occur to him to weigh and measure every proceeding, every practice which he meets with among those whom he has joined. He comes to Catholicism as to a living system, with a living teaching, and not to a mere collection of decrees and canons, which by themselves are of course but the framework, not the body and substance of the Church. And this is a truth which concerns, which binds, those also who never knew any other religion, not only the convert. By the Catholic system, I mean that rule of life, and those practices of devotion, for which we shall look in vain in the Creed of Pope Pius. The convert comes, not only to believe the Church, but also to trust and obey her priests, and to conform himself in charity to her people. It would never do for him to resolve that he never would say a Hail Mary, never avail himself of an indulgence, never kiss a crucifix, never accept the Lent dispensations, never mention a venial sin in confession. All this would not only be unreal, but dangerous too, as arguing a wrong state of mind, which could not look to receive the divine blessing. Moreover, he comes to the ceremonial, and the moral theology, and the ecclesiastical regulations, which he finds on the spot where his lot is cast. And again, as regards matters of politics, of education, of general expedience, of taste, he does not criticize or controvert. And thus surrendering himself to the influences of his new religion, and not risking the loss of revealed truth altogether by attempting by a private rule to discriminate every moment its substance from its accidents, he is gradually so indoctrinated in Catholicism, as at length to have a right to speak as well as to hear. Also in course of time a new generation rises round him; and there is no reason why he should not know as much, and decide questions with as true an instinct, as those who perhaps number fewer years than he does Easter communions. He has mastered the fact and the nature of the differences of theologian from theologian, school from school, nation from nation, era from era. He knows that there is much of what may be called fashion in opinions and practices, according to the circumstances of time and place, according to current politics, the character of the Pope of the day, or the chief Prelates of a particular country;—and that fashions change. His experience tells him, that sometimes what is denounced in one place as a great offence, or preached up as a first principle, has in another nation been immemorially regarded in just a contrary sense, or has made no sensation at all, one way or the other, when brought before public opinion; and that loud talkers, in the Church as elsewhere, are apt to carry all before them, while quiet and conscientious persons commonly have to give way. He perceives that, in matters which happen to be in debate, ecclesiastical authority watches the state of opinion and the direction and course of controversy, and decides accordingly; so that in certain cases to keep back his own judgment on a point, is to be disloyal to his superiors.

So far generally; now in particular as to myself. After twenty years of Catholic life, I feel no delicacy in giving my opinion on any point when there is a call for me,—and the only reason why I have not done so sooner or more often than I have, is that there has been no call. I have now reluctantly come to the conclusion that your Volume *is* a call. Certainly, in many instances in which theologian differs from theologian, and country from country, I have a definite judgment of my own; I can say so without offence to any one, for the very reason that from the nature of the case it is impossible to agree with all of them. I prefer English habits of belief and devotion to foreign, from the same causes, and by the same right, which justifies foreigners in preferring their own. In following those of my people, I show less singularity, and create less disturbance than if I made a flourish with what is novel and exotic. And in this line of conduct I am but availing myself of the teaching which I fell in with on becoming a Catholic; and it is a pleasure to me to think that what I hold now, and would transmit after me if I could, is only what I received then. The utmost delicacy was observed on all hands in giving me advice: only one warning remains on my mind, and it came from Dr. Griffiths, the late Vicar-Apostolic of the London district. He warned me against books of devotion of the Italian school, which were just at that time coming into England; and when I asked him what books he recommended as safe guides, he bade me get the works of Bishop Hay. By this I did not understand that he was jealous of all Italian books, or made himself responsible for all that Dr. Hay happens to have said; but I took him to caution me against a character and tone of religion, excellent in its place, not suited for England. When I went to Rome, though it may seem strange to you to say it, even there I learned nothing inconsistent with this judgment. Local influences do not form the atmosphere of its institutions and colleges, which are Catholic in teaching as well as in name. I recollect one saying among others of my confessor, a Jesuit father, one of the holiest, most prudent men I ever knew. He said that we could not love the Blessed Virgin too much, if we loved our Lord a great deal more. When I returned to England, the first expression of theological opinion which came in my way, was *apropos* of the series of translated Saints' Lives which the late Dr. Faber originated. That expression proceeded from a wise prelate, who was properly anxious as to the line which might be taken by the Oxford converts, then for the first time coming into work. According as I recollect his opinion, he was apprehensive of the effect of Italian compositions, as unsuited to this country, and suggested that the Lives should be original works, drawn up by ourselves and our friends from Italian sources. If at that time I was betrayed into any acts which were of a more extreme character than I should approve now, the responsibility of course is mine; but the impulse came, not from old Catholics or superiors, but from men whom I loved and trusted, who were younger than myself. But to whatever extent I might be carried away, and I cannot recollect any tangible instances, my mind in no long time fell back to what seems to me a safer and more practical course.

Though I am a convert, then, I think I have a right to speak out; and that the more because other converts have spoken for a long time, while I have not spoken; and with still more reason may I speak without offence in the case of your present criticisms of us, considering that, in the charges you bring, the only two English writers you quote in evidence, are both of them converts, younger in age than myself. I put aside the Archbishop of course, because of his office. These two authors are worthy of all consideration, at once from their character and from their ability. In their respective lines they are perhaps without equals at this particular time; and they deserve the influence they possess. One is still in the vigour of his powers; the other has departed amid the tears of hundreds. It is pleasant to praise them for their real excellencies; but why do you rest on them as authorities? You say of the one that he was " a popular writer;" but is there not sufficient reason for this in the fact of his remarkable gifts, of his poetical fancy, his engaging frankness, his playful wit, his affectionateness, his sensitive piety, without supposing that the wide diffusion of his works arises out of his particular sentiments about the Blessed Virgin? And as to our other friend, do not his energy, acuteness, and theological reading, displayed on the vantage ground of the historic "Dublin Review," fully account for the sensation he has produced, without supposing that any great number of our body go his lengths in their view of the Pope's infallibility? Our silence as regards their writings is very intelligible: it is not agreeable to protest, in the sight of the world, against the writings of men in our own communion whom we love and respect. But the plain fact is this,—they came to the Church, and have thereby saved their souls; but they are in no sense spokesmen for English Catholics, and they must not stand in the place of those who have a real title to such an office. The chief authors of the passing generation, some of them still alive, others gone to their reward, are Cardinal Wiseman, Dr. Ullathorne, Dr. Lingard, Mr. Tierney, Dr. Oliver, Dr. Rock, Dr. Waterworth, Dr. Husenbeth, and Mr. Flanagan; which of these ecclesiastics has said any thing extreme about the prerogatives of the Blessed Virgin or the infallibility of the Pope?

I cannot, then, without remonstrance, allow you to identify the doctrine of our Oxford friends in question, on the two subjects I have mentioned, with the present spirit or the prospective creed of Catholics; or to assume, as you do, that, because they are thorough-going and relentless in their

statements, therefore they are the harbingers of a
new age, when to show a deference for Antiquity
will be thought little else than a mistake. For
myself, hopeless as you consider it, I am not
ashamed still to take my stand upon the Fathers,
and do not mean to budge. The history of their
times is not yet an old almanac to me. Of course I
maintain the value and authority of the "Schola,"
as one of the *loci theologici;* still I sympathize with
Petavius in preferring to its "contentious and
subtle theology," that "more elegant and fruitful
teaching which is moulded after the image of
erudite antiquity." The Fathers made me a Catholic, and I am not going to kick down the ladder
by which I ascended into the Church. It is a
ladder quite as serviceable for that purpose now
as it was twenty years ago. Though I hold, as
you know, a process of development in Apostolic
truth as time goes on, such development does not
supersede the Fathers, but explains and completes
them. And, in particular, as regards our teaching
concerning the Blessed Virgin, with the Fathers I
am content;—and to the subject of that teaching I
mean to address myself at once. I do so, because
you say, as I myself have said in former years, that
" That vast system as to the Blessed Virgin . . . .
to all of us has been the special *crux* of the Roman
system."—P. 101. Here, I say, as on other points,
the Fathers are enough for me. I do not wish to
say more than they, and will not say less. You, I

know, will profess the same; and thus we can join issue on a clear and broad principle, and may hope to come to some intelligible result. We are to have a Treatise on the subject of our Lady soon from the pen of the Most Reverend Prelate; but that cannot interfere with such a mere argument from the Fathers as that to which I shall confine myself here. Nor indeed, as regards that argument itself, do I profess to be offering you any new matter, any facts which have not been used by others,—by great divines, as Petavius, by living writers, nay, by myself on other occasions; I write afresh nevertheless, and that for three reasons; first, because I wish to contribute to the accurate statement and the full exposition of the argument in question; next, because I may gain a more patient hearing than has sometimes been granted to better men than myself; lastly, because there just now seems a call on me, under my circumstances, to avow plainly what I do and what I do not hold about the Blessed Virgin, that others may know, did they come to stand where I stand, what they would and what they would not be bound to hold concerning her.

I BEGIN by making a distinction which will go far to remove good part of the difficulty of my undertaking, as it presents itself to ordinary inquirers,—the distinction between faith and devotion. I fully grant that *devotion* towards the Blessed Virgin has increased among Catholics with the progress of centuries; I do not allow that the *doctrine* concerning her has undergone a growth, for I believe that it has been in substance one and the same from the beginning.

By "faith" I mean the Creed and the acceptance of the Creed; by "devotion" I mean such religious honours as belong to the objects of our faith, and the payment of those honours. Faith and devotion are as distinct in fact as they are in idea. We cannot, indeed, be devout without faith, but we may believe without feeling devotion. Of this phenomenon every one has experience both in himself and in others; and we express it as often as we speak of realizing a truth or not realizing it. It may be illustrated, with more or less exactness, by matters which come before us in the world. For instance, a great author, or public man, may be acknowledged as such for a course of years; yet there may be an increase, an ebb and flow, and a fashion, in his popularity. And if he takes a lasting place in the minds of his countrymen, he may gradually grow into it, or suddenly be raised to it. The idea of Shakespeare as a great poet, has existed from a very early date in public opinion; and there were at least individuals then who understood him as well, and honoured him as much, as the English people can honour him now; yet, I think, there is a national devotion to him in this day such as never has been before. This has happened, because, as education spreads in the country, there are more men able to enter into his poetical genius, and, among these, more capacity again for deeply and critically understanding him; and yet, from the first, he has exerted a great insensible influence over the nation, as is seen in the circumstance that his phrases and sentences, more than can be numbered, have become almost proverbs among us. And so again in philosophy, and in the arts and sciences, great truths and principles have sometimes been known and acknowledged for a course of years; but, whether from feebleness of intellectual power in the recipients, or external circumstances of an accidental kind, they have not been turned to account. Thus the Chinese are said to have known of the properties of the magnet from time immemorial, and to have used it for land expeditions, yet not on the sea. Again, the ancients knew of the principle that water finds its own level, but seem to have made little application of their knowledge. And Aristotle was familiar with the principle of induction; yet it was left for Bacon to develope it into an experimental philosophy. Illustrations such as these, though not altogether apposite, serve to convey that distinction between faith and devotion on which I am insisting. It is like the distinction between objective and subjective truth. The sun in the spring-time will have to shine many days before he is able to melt the frost, open the soil, and bring out the leaves; yet he shines out from the first, notwithstanding, though he makes his power felt but gradually. It is one and the same sun, though his influence day by day becomes greater; and so in the Catholic Church it is the one Virgin Mother, one and the same from first to last, and Catholics may acknowledge her; and yet, in spite of that acknowledgment, their devotion to her may be scanty in one time and place, and overflowing in another.

This distinction is forcibly brought home to a convert, as a peculiarity of the Catholic religion, on his first introduction to its worship. The faith is every where one and the same; but a large liberty is accorded to private judgment and inclination in matters of devotion. Any large church, with its collections and groups of people, will illustrate this. The fabric itself is dedicated to Almighty God, and that, under the invocation of the Blessed Virgin, or some particular Saint; or again, of some mystery belonging to the Divine Name or to the Incarnation, or of some mystery associated with the Blessed Virgin. Perhaps there are seven altars or more in it, and these again have their several Saints. Then there is the Feast proper to the particular day; and, during the celebration of Mass, of all the worshippers who crowd around the Priest, each has his own particular devotions, with which he follows the rite. No one interferes with his neighbour; agreeing, as it were, to differ, they pursue independently a common end, and by paths, distinct but converging, present themselves before God. Then there are Confraternities attached to the church,—of the Sacred Heart, or the Precious Blood; associations of prayer for a good death, or the repose of departed souls, or the conversion of the heathen; devotions connected with the brown, blue, or red scapular;—not to speak of the great ordinary Ritual through the four seasons, the constant Presence of the Blessed Sacrament, its ever-recurring rite of Benediction, and its extraordinary forty hours' Exposition. Or, again, look through some such manual of prayers as the *Raccolta*, and you at once will see both the number and the variety of devotions, which are open to individual Catholics to choose from, according to their religious taste and prospect of personal edification.

Now these diversified modes of honouring God did not come to us in a day, or only from the Apostles; they are the accumulations of centuries;

and, as in the course of years some of them spring up, so others decline and die. Some are local, in memory of some particular saint, who happens to be the Evangelist, or Patron, or pride of the nation, or who is entombed in the church, or in the city where it stands; and these, necessarily, cannot have an earlier date than the Saint's day of death or interment there. The first of such sacred observances, long before these national memories, were the devotions paid to the Apostles, then those which were paid to the Martyrs; yet there were Saints nearer to our Lord than either Martyrs or Apostles; but, as if these had been lost in the effulgence of His glory, and because they were not manifested in external works separate from Him, it happened that for a long while they were less dwelt upon. However, in process of time, the Apostles, and then the Martyrs, exerted less influence than before over the popular mind, and the local Saints, new creations of God's power, took their place, or again, the Saints of some religious order here or there established. Then, as comparatively quiet times succeeded, the religious meditations of holy men and their secret intercourse with heaven gradually exerted an influence out of doors, and permeated the Christian populace, by the instrumentality of preaching and by the ceremonial of the Church. Then those luminous stars rose in the ecclesiastical heavens, which were of more august dignity than any which had preceded them, and were late in rising, for the very reason that they were so specially glorious. Those names, I say, which at first sight might have been expected to enter soon into the devotions of the faithful, with better reason might have been looked for at a later date, and actually were late in their coming. St. Joseph furnishes the most striking instance of this remark; here is the clearest of instances of the distinction between doctrine and devotion. Who, from his prerogatives and the testimony on which they come to us, had a greater claim to receive an early recognition among the faithful? A saint of Scripture, the foster-father of our Lord, he was an object of the universal and absolute faith of the Christian world from the first, yet the devotion to him is comparatively of late date. When once it began, men seemed surprised that it had not been thought of before; and now, they hold him next to the Blessed Virgin in their religious affection and veneration.

As regards the Blessed Virgin, I shall postpone the question of devotion for a while, and inquire first into the doctrine of the undivided Church (to use your controversial phrase), on the subject of her prerogatives.

What is the great rudimental teaching of Antiquity from its earliest date concerning her? By "rudimental teaching" I mean the *primâ facie* view of her person and office, the broad outline laid down of her, the aspect under which she comes to us, in the writings of the Fathers. She is the Second Eve[1]. Now let us consider what this implies. Eve had a definite, essential position in the First Covenant. The fate of the human race lay with Adam; he it was who represented us. It was in Adam that we fell; though Eve had fallen, still, if Adam had stood, we should not have lost those supernatural privileges which were bestowed upon him as our first father. Yet though Eve was not the head of the race, still, even as regards the race, she had a place of her own; for Adam, to whom was divinely committed the naming of all things, entitled her "the Mother of all the living," a name surely expressive, not of a fact only, but of a dignity; but further, as she thus had her own general relation to the human race, so again had she her own special place, as regards its trial and its fall in Adam. In those primeval events, Eve had an integral share. "The woman, being seduced, was in the transgression." She listened to the Evil Angel; she offered the fruit to her husband, and he ate of it. She co-operated, not as an irresponsible instrument, but intimately and personally in the sin: she brought it about. As the history stands, she was a *sine-qua-non*, a positive, active, cause of it. And she had her share in its punishment; in the sentence pronounced on her, she was recognized as a real agent in the temptation and its issue,

---

[1] Vid. Essay on Development of Doctrine, 1845, p. 384, &c.

and she suffered accordingly. In that awful transaction there were three parties concerned,—the serpent, the woman, and the man; and at the time of their sentence, an event was announced for the future, in which the three same parties were to meet again, the serpent, the woman, and the man; but it was to be a second Adam and a second Eve, and the new Eve was to be the mother of the new Adam. "I will put enmity between thee and the woman, and between thy seed and her seed." The Seed of the woman is the Word Incarnate, and the Woman, whose seed or son He is, is His mother Mary. This interpretation, and the parallelism it involves, seem to me undeniable; but at all events (and this is my point) the parallelism is the doctrine of the Fathers, from the earliest times; and, this being established, we are able, by the position and office of Eve in our fall, to determine the position and office of Mary in our restoration.

I shall adduce passages from their writings, with their respective countries and dates; and the dates shall extend from their births or conversions to their deaths, since what they propound is at once the doctrine which they had received from the generation before them, and the doctrine which was accepted and recognized as true by the generation to whom they transmitted it.

First then St. Justin Martyr (A.D. 120—165), St. Irenæus (120—200) and Tertullian (160—240). Of these Tertullian represents Africa and Rome;

St. Justin represents Palestine; and St. Irenæus Asia Minor and Gaul;—or rather he represents St. John the Evangelist, for he had been taught by the Martyr St. Polycarp, who was the intimate associate, as of St. John, so of the other Apostles.

1. St. Justin [2]:—

"We know that He, before all creatures, proceeded from the Father by His power and will, . . . and by means of the Virgin became man, that by what way the disobedience arising from the serpent had its beginning, by that way also it might have an undoing. For Eve, being a virgin and undefiled, conceiving the word that was from the serpent, brought forth disobedience and death; but the Virgin Mary, taking faith and joy, when the Angel told her the good tidings, that the Spirit of the Lord should come upon her and the power of the Highest, overshadow her, and therefore the Holy One that was born of her was Son of God, answered, Be it to me according to thy word."—*Tryph.* 100.

2. Tertullian:—

"God recovered His image and likeness, which the devil had seized, by a rival operation. For into Eve, as yet a virgin, had crept the word which was the framer of death. Equally into a virgin was to be introduced the Word of God which was the builder-up of life; that, what by that sex had gone into perdition, by the same sex might be brought back to salvation. Eve had believed the serpent; Mary believed Gabriel; the fault which the one committed by believing, the other by believing has blotted out."—*De Carn. Christ.* 17.

3. St. Irenæus:—

"With a fitness, Mary the Virgin is found obedient, saying,

---

[2] I have attempted to translate literally without caring to write English. The original passages are at the end of the Letter.

'Behold Thy handmaid, O Lord; be it to me according to thy word.' But Eve was disobedient; for she obeyed not, while she was yet a virgin. As she, having indeed Adam for a husband, but as yet being a virgin.... becoming disobedient, became the cause of death both to herself and to the whole human race, so also Mary, having the predestined man, and being yet a virgin, being obedient, became both to herself and to the whole human race the cause of salvation.... And on account of this the Lord said, that the first would be last and the last first. And the Prophet signifies the same, saying, 'Instead of fathers you have children.' For, whereas the Lord, when born, was the first begotten of the dead, and received into His bosom the primitive fathers, He regenerated them into the life of God, He Himself becoming the beginning of the living, since Adam became the beginning of the dying. Therefore also Luke, commencing the lines of generations from the Lord referred it back to Adam, signifying that He regenerated the old fathers, not they Him, into the Gospel of life. And so the knot of Eve's disobedience received its unloosing through the obedience of Mary; for what Eve, a virgin, bound by incredulity, that Mary, a virgin, unloosed by faith."—*Adv. Hær.* iii. 22. 34.

And again,—

"As Eve by the speech of an Angel was seduced, so as to flee God, transgressing His word, so also Mary received the good tidings by means of the Angel's speech, so as to bear God within her, being obedient to His word. And, though the one had disobeyed God, yet the other was drawn to obey God; that of the virgin Eve the virgin Mary might become the advocate. And, as by a virgin the human race had been bound to death, by a virgin it is saved, the balance being preserved, a virgin's disobedience by a virgin's obedience."— *Ibid.* v. 19.

Now, what is especially noticeable in these three writers, is, that they do not speak of the Blessed Virgin merely as the physical instrument of our

Lord's taking flesh, but as an intelligent, responsible cause of it; her faith and obedience being accessories to the Incarnation, and gaining it as her reward. As Eve failed in these virtues, and thereby brought on the fall of the race in Adam, so Mary by means of them had a part in its restoration. You surely imply, pp. 255, 256, that the Blessed Virgin was only a physical instrument in our redemption; "what has been said of her by the Fathers as the chosen *vessel* of the Incarnation, was applied *personally* to her," (that is, by Catholics,) p. 151, and again "the Fathers speak of the Blessed Virgin as the *instrument* of our salvation, *in that* she gave birth to the Redeemer," pp. 155, 156; whereas St. Augustine, in well-known passages, speaks of her as more exalted by her sanctity than by her relationship to our Lord[3]. However, not to go beyond the doctrine of the Three Fathers, they unanimously declare that she was *not* a mere instrument in the Incarnation, such as David, or Judah, may be considered; they declare she co-operated in our salvation, not merely by the descent of the Holy Ghost upon her body, but by specific holy acts, the effect of the Holy Ghost within her soul; that, as Eve forfeited privileges by sin, so Mary earned privileges by the fruits of grace; that, as Eve was disobedient and unbelieving, so Mary was obedient and believing; that, as Eve was a cause of ruin to all, Mary was a

---

[3] Opp. t. 3, p. 2, col. 369, t. 6, col. 342.

cause of salvation to all; that as Eve made room for Adam's fall, so Mary made room for our Lord's reparation of it; and thus, whereas the free gift was not as the offence, but much greater, it follows that, as Eve co-operated in effecting a great evil, Mary co-operated in effecting a much greater good.

And, besides the run of the argument, which reminds the reader of St. Paul's antithetical sentences in tracing the analogy between Adam's work and our Lord's work, it is well to observe the particular words under which the Blessed Virgin's office is described. Tertullian says that Mary "blotted out" Eve's fault, and "brought back the female sex," or "the human race, to salvation;" and St. Irenæus says that "by obedience she was the cause or occasion" (whatever was the original Greek word) "of salvation to herself and the whole human race;" that by her the human race is saved; that by her Eve's complication is disentangled; and that she is Eve's Advocate, or friend in need. It is supposed by critics, Protestant as well as Catholic, that the Greek word for Advocate in the original was Paraclete; it should be borne in mind, then, when we are accused of giving our Lady the titles and offices of her Son, that St. Irenæus bestows on her the special Name and office proper to the Holy Ghost.

So much as to the nature of this triple testimony; now as to the worth of it. For a moment put aside St. Irenæus, and put together St. Justin

in the East with Tertullian in the West. I think
I may assume that the doctrine of these two
Fathers about the Blessed Virgin, was the received
doctrine of their own respective times and places;
for writers after all are but witnesses of facts and
beliefs, and as such they are treated by all parties
in controversial discussion. Moreover, the coinci-
dence of doctrine which they exhibit, and again,
the antithetical completeness of it, show that they
themselves did not originate it. The next question
is, Who did? for from one definite organ or
source, place or person, it must have come. Then
we must inquire, what length of time would it take
for such a doctrine to have extended, and to be
received, in the second century over so wide an
area; that is, to be received before the year 200 in
Palestine, Africa, and Rome. Can we refer the
common source of these local traditions to a date
later than that of the Apostles, St. John dying
within thirty or forty years of St. Justin's conversion and Tertullian's birth? Make what allowance
you will for whatever possible exceptions can be
taken to this representation; and then, after doing
so, add to the concordant testimony of these two
Fathers the evidence of St. Irenæus, which is so
close upon the School of St. John himself in Asia
Minor. "A three-fold cord," as the wise man
says, "is not quickly broken." Only suppose there
were so early and so broad a testimony, to the effect
that our Lord was a mere man, the son of Joseph;

should we be able to insist upon the faith of the Holy Trinity as necessary to salvation? Or supposing three such witnesses could be brought to the fact that a consistory of elders governed the local churches, or that each local congregation was an independent Church, or that the Christian community was without priests, could Anglicans maintain their doctrine that the rule of Episcopal succession is necessary to constitute a Church? And then recollect that the Anglican Church especially appeals to the ante-Nicene centuries, and taunts us with having superseded their testimony.

Having then adduced these Three Fathers of the second century, I have at least got so far as this: viz.—no one, who acknowledges the force of early testimony in determining Christian truth, can wonder, no one can complain, can object, that we Catholics should hold a very high doctrine concerning the Blessed Virgin, unless indeed stronger statements can be brought for a contrary conception of her, either of as early, or at least of a later date. But, as far as I know, no statements can be brought from the ante-Nicene literature, to invalidate the testimony of the three Fathers concerning her; and little can be brought against it from the fourth century, while in that fourth century the current of testimony in her behalf is as strong as in the second; and, as to the fifth, it is far stronger than in any former time, both in its fulness and its authority. This will to some extent be seen as I proceed.

4. St. Cyril of Jerusalem (315—386) speaks for Palestine:—

"Since through Eve, a Virgin, came death, it behoved, that through a Virgin, or rather from a Virgin, should life appear; that, as the Serpent had deceived the one, so to the other Gabriel might bring good tidings."—*Cat.* xii. 15.

5. St. Ephrem Syrus (he died 378) is a witness for the Syrians proper and the neighbouring Orientals, in contrast to the Græco-Syrians. A native of Nisibis on the further side of the Euphrates, he knew no language but Syriac.

" Through Eve, the beautiful and desirable glory of men was extinguished: but it has revived through Mary."—*Opp. Syr.* ii. p. 318.

Again:—

"In the beginning, by the sin of our first parents, death passed upon all men; to-day, through Mary we are translated from death unto life. In the beginning, the serpent filled the ears of Eve, and the poison spread thence over the whole body; to-day, Mary from her ears received the champion of eternal happiness: what, therefore, was an instrument of death, was an instrument of life also."—iii. p. 607.

I have already referred to St. Paul's contrast between Adam and our Lord in his Epistle to the Romans, as also in his first Epistle to the Corinthians. Some writers venture to say that there is no doctrinal truth, but a mere rhetorical display, in those passages. It is quite as easy to say so, as to attempt so to dispose of this received comparison, in the writings of the Fathers, between Eve and Mary.

6. St. Epiphanius (320—400) speaks for Egypt, Palestine, and Cyprus:—

"She it is, who is signified by Eve, enigmatically receiving the appellation of the Mother of the living..... It was a wonder that after the transgression she had this great epithet. And, according to what is material, from that Eve all the race of men on earth is generated. But thus in truth from Mary the Life itself was born in the world, that Mary might bear living things, and become the Mother of living things. Therefore, enigmatically, Mary is called the Mother of living things ... Also, there is another thing to consider as to these women, and wonderful, — as to Eve and Mary. Eve became a cause of death to man .... and Mary a cause of life; ... that life might be instead of death, life excluding death which came from the woman, viz. He who through the woman has become our life."—*Hær*. 78. 18.

7. By the time of St. Jerome (331—420), the contrast between Eve and Mary had almost passed into a proverb. He says (*Ep.* xxii. 21, *ad Eustoch.*), "Death by Eve, life by Mary." Nor let it be supposed that he, any more than the preceding Fathers, considered the Blessed Virgin a mere physical instrument of giving birth to our Lord, who is the Life. So far from it, in the Epistle from which I have quoted, he is only adding another virtue to that crown which gained for Mary her divine Maternity. They have spoken of faith, joy, and obedience; St. Jerome adds, what they had only suggested, virginity. After the manner of the Fathers in his own day, he is setting forth the

Blessed Mary to the high-born Roman Lady, whom he is addressing, as the model of the virginal life; and his argument in its behalf is, that it is higher than the marriage-state, not in itself, viewed in any mere natural respect, but as being the free act of self-consecration to God, and from the personal religious purpose, which it involves.

"Higher wage," he says, "is due to that which is not a compulsion, but an offering; for, were virginity commanded, marriage would seem to be put out of the question; and it would be most cruel to force men against nature, and to extort from them an angel's life."—20.

I do not know whose testimony is more important than St. Jerome's, the friend of Pope Damasus at Rome, the pupil of St. Gregory Nazianzen at Constantinople, and of Didymus in Alexandria, a native of Dalmatia, yet an inhabitant, at different times of his life, of Gaul, Syria, and Palestine.

8. St. Jerome speaks for the whole world, except Africa; and for Africa in the fourth century, if we must limit so world-wide an authority to place, witnesses St. Augustine (354—430). He repeats the words as if a proverb, "By a woman death, by a woman life" (*Opp. t.* v. *Serm.* 232); elsewhere he enlarges on the idea conveyed in it. In one place he quotes St. Irenæus's words, as cited above (*adv. Julian* i. 4). In another he speaks as follows:—

"It is a great sacrament that, whereas through woman death became our portion, so life was born to us by woman; that, in the case of both sexes, male and female, the baffled devil should be tormented, when on the overthrow of both sexes he was rejoicing; whose punishment had been small, if both sexes had been liberated in us, without our being liberated through both."—*Opp. t.* vi. *De Agon. Christ.* c. 24.

9. St. Peter Chrysologus (400—450), Bishop of Ravenna, and one of the chief authorities in the 4th General Council:—

"Blessed art thou among women; for among women, on whose womb Eve, who was cursed, brought punishment, Mary, being blest, rejoices, is honoured, and is looked up to. And woman now is truly made through grace the Mother of the living, who had been by nature the mother of the dying. . . . . Heaven feels awe of God, Angels tremble at Him, the creature sustains Him not, nature sufficeth not; and yet one maiden so takes, receives, entertains Him, as a guest within her breast, that, for the very hire of her home, and as the price of her womb, she asks, she obtains peace for the earth, glory for the heavens, salvation for the lost, life for the dead, a heavenly parentage for the earthly, the union of God Himself with human flesh."—*Serm.* 140.

It is difficult to express more explicitly, though in oratorical language, that the Blessed Virgin had a real meritorious co-operation, a share which had a "hire" and a "price," in the reversal of the fall.

10. St. Fulgentius, Bishop of Ruspe in Africa (468—533). The Homily which contains the following passage, is placed by Ceillier (t. xvi. p. 127), among his genuine works:—

"In the wife of the first man, the wickedness of the devil depraved her seduced mind; in the mother of the Second Man, the grace of God preserved both her mind inviolate and her flesh. On her mind it conferred the most firm faith; from her flesh it took away lust altogether. Since then man was in a miserable way condemned for sin, therefore without sin was in a marvellous way born the God man."—*Serm.* 2, p. 124. *De Dupl. Nativ.*

Accordingly, in the Sermon which follows (if it is his), he continues, illustrating her office of universal Mother, as ascribed to her by St. Epiphanius:—

" Come ye virgins to a Virgin, come ye who conceive to her who conceived, ye who bear to one who bore, mothers to a mother, ye that suckle to one who suckled, young girls to the young girl. It is for this reason that the Virgin Mary has taken on her in our Lord Jesus Christ all these divisions of nature, that to all women who have recourse to her, she may be a succour, and so restore the whole race of women who come to her, being the new Eve, by keeping virginity, as the new Adam, the Lord Jesus Christ, recovers the whole race of men."

Such is the rudimental view, as I have called it, which the Fathers have given us of Mary, as the Second Eve, the Mother of the living: I have cited ten authors. I could cite more, were it necessary: except the two last, they write gravely and without any rhetoric. I allow that the two last write in a different style, since the extracts I have made are from their sermons; but I do not see that the colouring conceals the outline. And after all, men use oratory on great subjects, not on small;—nor would they, and other Fathers whom I might quote, have lavished their high language upon the Blessed Virgin, such as they gave to no one else, unless they knew well that no one else had such claims, as she had, on their love and veneration.

And now, I proceed to dwell for a while upon two inferences, which it is obvious to draw from the rudimental doctrine itself; the first relates to the sanctity of the Blessed Virgin, the second to her greatness.

1. Her sanctity. She holds, as the Fathers teach us, that office in our restoration which Eve held in our fall:—now in the first place what were Eve's endowments to enable her to enter upon her trial? She could not have stood against the wiles of the devil, though she was innocent and sinless, without the grant of a large grace. And this she had;—a heavenly gift, which was over and above and additional to that nature of hers, which she received from Adam, as Adam before her had also received the same gift, at the very time (as it is commonly held) of his original creation. This is Anglican doctrine as well as Catholic; it is the doctrine of Bishop Bull. He has written a dissertation on the point. He speaks of the doctrine which "many of the Schoolmen affirm, that Adam was created in grace, that is, received a principle of grace and divine life from his very creation, or in the moment of the infusion of his soul; of which," he says, "for my own part I have little doubt." Again, he says, "It is abundantly manifest from the many testimonies alleged, that the ancient doctors of the Church did, with a general consent, acknowledge, that our first parents in the state of integrity, had in them something more

than nature, that is, were endowed with the divine principle of the Spirit, in order to a supernatural felicity."

Now, taking this for granted, because I know that you and those who agree with you maintain it as well as we do, I ask, was not Mary as fully endowed as Eve? is it any violent inference, that she, who was to co-operate in the redemption of the world, at least was not less endowed with power from on high, than she who, given as a helpmate to her husband, did in the event but co-operate with him for its ruin. If Eve was raised above human nature by that indwelling moral gift which we call grace, is it rash to say that Mary had a greater grace? And this consideration gives significance to the Angel's salutation of her as "full of grace,"—an interpretation of the original word which is undoubtedly the right one, as soon as we resist the common Protestant assumption that grace is a mere external approbation or acceptance, answering to the word "favour," whereas it is, as the Fathers teach, a real inward condition or superadded quality of soul. And if Eve had this supernatural inward gift given her from the first moment of her personal existence, is it possible to deny that Mary too had this gift from the very first moment of her personal existence? I do not know how to resist this inference:—well, this is simply and literally the doctrine of the Immaculate Conception. I say the doctrine of the Immaculate Conception is in its substance this, and nothing more or less than this (putting aside the question of degrees of grace); and it really does seem to me bound up in that doctrine of the Fathers, that Mary is the second Eve.

It is to me a most strange phenomenon that so many learned and devout men stumble at this doctrine, and I can only account for it by supposing that in matter of fact they do not know what we mean by the Immaculate Conception; and your Volume (may I say it?) bears out my suspicion. It is a great consolation to have reason for thinking so,—for believing that in some sort the persons in question are in the position of those great Saints in former times, who are said to have hesitated about it, when they would not have hesitated at all, if the word "Conception" had been clearly explained in that sense in which now it is universally received. I do not see how any one who holds with Bull the Catholic doctrine of the supernatural endowments of our first parents, has fair reason for doubting our doctrine about the Blessed Virgin. It has no reference whatever to her parents, but simply to her own person; it does but affirm that, together with the nature which she inherited from her parents, that is, her own nature, she had a super-added fulness of grace, and that from the first moment of her existence. Suppose Eve had stood the trial, and not lost her first grace; and suppose she had eventually had children, those children from the first moment of their existence would, through divine bounty, have received the same privilege that she had ever had; that is, as she was taken from Adam's side, in a garment, so to say, of grace, so they in turn would have received what may be called an immaculate conception. They would have been conceived in grace, as in fact they are conceived in sin. What is there difficult in this doctrine? What is there unnatural? Mary may be called a daughter of Eve unfallen. You believe with us that St. John Baptist had grace given to him three months before his birth, at the time that the Blessed Virgin visited his mother. He accordingly was *not* immaculately conceived, because he was alive before grace came to him; but our Lady's case only differs from his in this respect, that to her grace came, not three months merely before her birth, but from the first moment of her being, as it had been given to Eve.

But it may be said, How does this enable us to say that she was conceived without *original sin*? If Anglicans knew what we mean by original sin, they would not ask the question. Our doctrine of original sin is not the same as the Protestant doctrine. "Original sin," with us, cannot be called sin, in the ordinary sense of the word "sin;" it is a term denoting Adam's sin as transferred to us, or the state to which Adam's sin reduces his children; but by Protestants it is understood to be sin, in the same sense as actual sin. We, with the

Fathers, think of it as something negative, Protestants as something positive. Protestants hold that it is a disease, a radical change of nature, an active poison internally corrupting the soul, infecting its primary elements, and disorganizing it; and they fancy that we ascribe a different nature from ours to the Blessed Virgin, different from that of her parents, and from that of fallen Adam. We hold nothing of the kind; we consider that in Adam she died, as others; that she was included, together with the whole race, in Adam's sentence; that she incurred his debt, as we do; but that, for the sake of Him who was to redeem her and us upon the Cross, to her the debt was remitted by anticipation, on her the sentence was not carried out, except indeed as regards her natural death, for she died when her time came, as others. All this we teach, but we deny that she had original sin; for by original sin we mean, as I have already said, something negative, viz., this only, the *deprivation* of that supernatural unmerited grace which Adam and Eve had on their creation,—deprivation and the consequences of deprivation. Mary could not merit, any more than they, the restoration of that grace; but it was restored to her by God's free bounty, from the very first moment of her existence, and thereby, in fact, she never came under the original curse, which consisted in the loss of it. And she had this special privilege, in order to fit her to become the Mother of her and our Redeemer, to fit her mentally, spiritually for it; so that, by the aid of the first grace, she might so grow in grace, that when the Angel came, and her Lord was at hand, she might be "full of grace," prepared, as far as a creature could be prepared, to receive Him into her bosom.

I have drawn the doctrine of the Immaculate Conception, as an immediate inference, from the primitive doctrine that Mary is the second Eve. The argument seems to me conclusive; and, if it has not been universally taken as such, this has come to pass, because there has not been a clear understanding among Catholics, what exactly was meant by the Immaculate Conception. To many it seemed to imply that the Blessed Virgin did not die in Adam, that she did not come under the penalty of the fall, that she was not redeemed, that she was conceived in some way inconsistent with the verse in the *Miserere* Psalm. If controversy had in earlier days so cleared the subject as to make it plain to all, that the doctrine meant nothing else than that in fact in her case the general sentence on mankind was not carried out, and that, by means of the indwelling in her of divine grace from the first moment of her being (and this is all the decree of 1854 has declared), I cannot believe that the doctrine would have ever been opposed; for an instinctive sentiment has led Christians jealously to put the Blessed Mary aside when sin comes into discussion.

This is expressed in the well-known words of St. Augustine, All have sinned "except the Holy Virgin Mary, concerning whom, for the honour of the Lord, I wish no question to be raised at all, when we are treating of sins" (*de Nat. et Grat.* 42); words which, whatever St. Augustine's actual occasion of using them, (to which you refer, p. 176,) certainly in the spirit which they breathe, are well adapted to convey the notion, that, apart from her relation to her parents, she had not personally any part in sin whatever. It is true that several great Fathers of the fourth century do imply or assert that on one or two occasions she did sin venially or showed infirmity. This is the only real objection which I know of; and as I do not wish to pass it over lightly, I propose to consider it at the end of this Letter.

2. Now secondly, her *greatness*. Here let us suppose that our first parents had overcome in their trial; and had gained for their descendants for ever the full possession, as if by right, of the privileges which were promised to their obedience,—grace here and glory hereafter. Is it possible that those descendants, pious and happy from age to age in their temporal homes, would have forgotten their benefactors? Would they not have followed them in thought into the heavens, and gratefully commemorated them on earth? The history of the temptation, the craft of the serpent, their sted-

fastness in obedience,—the loyal vigilance, the sensitive purity of Eve,—the great issue, salvation wrought out for all generations,—would have been never from their minds, ever welcome to their ears. This would have taken place from the necessity of our nature. Every nation has its mythical hymns and epics about its first fathers and its heroes. The great deeds of Charlemagne, Alfred, Cœur de Lion, Wallace, Louis the ninth, do not die; and though their persons are gone from us, we make much of their names. Milton's Adam, after his fall, understands the force of this law, and shrinks from the prospect of its operation.

> "Who of all ages to succeed, but, feeling
> The evil on him brought by me, will curse
> My head? Ill fare our ancestor impure,
> For this we may thank Adam."

If this anticipation has not been fulfilled in the event, it is owing to the needs of our penal life, our state of perpetual change, and the ignorance and unbelief incurred by the fall; also because, fallen as we are, from the hopefulness of our nature, we feel more pride in our national great men, than dejection at our national misfortunes. Much more then in the great kingdom and people of God;— the Saints are ever in our sight, and not as mere ineffectual ghosts, but as if present bodily in their past selves. It is said of them, "Their works do follow them;" what they were here, such are they in heaven and in the Church. As we call them by their earthly names, so we contemplate them in their earthly characters and histories. Their acts, callings, and relations below, are types and anticipations of their mission above. Even in the case of our Lord Himself, whose native home is the eternal heavens, it is said of Him in His state of glory, that He is "a Priest for ever;" and when He comes again, He will be recognized by those who pierced Him, as being the very same that He was on earth. The only question is, whether the Blessed Virgin had a part, a real part, in the economy of grace, whether, when she was on earth, she secured by her deeds any claim on our memories; for, if she did, it is impossible we should put her away from us, merely because she is gone hence, and not look at her still, according to the measure of her earthly history, with gratitude and expectation. If, as St. Irenæus says, she did the part of an Advocate, a friend in need, even in her mortal life, if, as St. Jerome and St. Ambrose say, she was on earth the great pattern of Virgins, if she had a meritorious share in bringing about our redemption, if her maternity was earned by her faith and obedience, if her Divine Son was subject to her, and if she stood by the Cross with a mother's heart and drank in to the full those sufferings which it was her portion to gaze upon, it is impossible that we should not associate these characteristics of her life on earth with her present state of blessedness; and this surely she anticipated, when she said in her hymn that "all generations should call her blessed."

I am aware that, in thus speaking, I am following a line of thought which is rather a meditation than an argument in controversy, and I shall not carry it further; but still, in turning to other topics, it is to the point to inquire, whether the popular astonishment, excited by our belief in the Blessed Virgin's present dignity, does not arise from the circumstance that the bulk of men, engaged in matters of the world, have never calmly considered her historical position in the gospels, so as rightly to realize (if I may use the word a second time) what that position imports. I do not claim for the generality of Catholics any greater powers of reflection upon the objects of their faith, than Protestants commonly have, but there is a sufficient number of religious men among Catholics who, instead of expending their devotional energies (as so many serious Protestants do) on abstract doctrines, such as justification by faith only, or the sufficiency of Holy Scripture, employ themselves in the contemplation of Scripture facts, and bring out in a tangible form the doctrines involved in them, and give such a substance and colour to the sacred history, as to influence their brethren; who, though superficial themselves, are drawn by their Catholic instinct to accept conclusions which they could not indeed themselves have elicited, but which, when elicited, they feel to be true. However, it would be out of place to pursue this course of reasoning here; and instead of doing so, I shall take what perhaps you may think a very bold step,—I shall find the doctrine of our Lady's present exaltation in Scripture.

I mean to find it in the vision of the Woman and Child in the twelfth chapter of the Apocalypse [4]:— now here two objections will be made to me at once; first that such an interpretation is but poorly supported by the Fathers, and secondly that in ascribing such a picture of the Madonna (as it may be called) to the Apostolic age, I am committing an anachronism.

As to the former of these objections, I answer as follows:—Christians have never gone to Scripture for proofs of their doctrines, till there was actual need, from the pressure of controversy;—if in those times the Blessed Virgin's dignity were unchallenged on all hands, as a matter of doctrine, Scripture, as far as its argumentative matter was concerned, was likely to remain a sealed book to them. Thus, to take an instance in point; the Catholic party in the English Church, (say, the Nonjurors,) unable by their theory of religion simply to take their stand on Tradition, and distressed for proof of their doctrines, had their eyes sharpened to scrutinize and to understand the letter of Holy

[4] Vid. Essay on Doctr. Development, p. 384, and Bishop Ullathorne's work on the Immaculate Conception, p. 77.

Scripture, which to others brought no instruction. And the peculiarity of their interpretations is this,—that they have in themselves great logical cogency, yet are but faintly supported by patristical commentators. Such is the use of the word ποιεῖν or *facere* in our Lord's institution of the Holy Eucharist, which, by a reference to the old Testament, is found to be a word of sacrifice. Such again is λειτουργούντων in the passage in the Acts, " As they *ministered* to the Lord and fasted," which again is a sacerdotal term. And such the passage in Rom. xv. 16, in which several terms are used which have an allusion to the sacrificial Eucharistic rite. Such too is St. Paul's repeated message to the *household* of Onesiphorus, with no mention of Onesiphorus himself, but in one place with the addition of a prayer that " he might find mercy of the Lord" in the day of judgment, which, taking into account its wording and the known usage of the first centuries, we can hardly deny is a prayer for his soul. Other texts there are, which ought to find a place in ancient controversies, and the omission of which by the Fathers affords matter for more surprise; those, for instance, which, according to Middleton's rule, are real proofs of our Lord's divinity, and yet are passed over by Catholic disputants; for these bear upon a then existing controversy of the first moment, and of the most urgent exigency.

As to the second objection which I have supposed, so far from allowing it, I consider that it is built upon a mere imaginary fact, and that the truth of the matter lies in the very contrary direction. The Virgin and Child is *not* a mere modern idea; on the contrary, it is represented again and again, as every visitor to Rome is aware, in the paintings of the Catacombs. Mary is there drawn with the Divine Infant in her lap, she with hands extended in prayer, He with His hand in the attitude of blessing. No representation can more forcibly convey the doctrine of the high dignity of the Mother, and, I will add, of her power over her Son. Why should the memory of His time of subjection be so dear to Christians, and so carefully preserved? The only question to be determined, is the precise date of these remarkable monuments of the first age of Christianity. That they belong to the centuries of what Anglicans call the "undivided Church" is certain; but lately investigations have been pursued, which place some of them at an earlier date than any one anticipated as possible. I am not in a position to quote largely from the works of the Cavaliere de Rossi, who has thrown so much light upon the subject; but I have his "Imagini Scelte," published in 1863, and they are sufficient for my purpose. In this work he has given us from the Catacombs various representations of the Virgin and Child; the latest of these belong to the early part of the fourth century, but the earliest he believes to be referable to the very age of the Apostles. He comes to this conclusion from the style and the skill of the composition, and from the history, locality, and existing inscriptions of the subterranean in which it is found. However he does not go so far as to insist upon so early a date; yet the utmost liberty he grants is to refer the painting to the era of the first Antonines, that is, to a date within half a century of the death of St. John. I consider then, that, as you fairly use, in controversy with Protestants, the traditional doctrine of the Church in early times, as an explanation of the Scripture text, or at least as a suggestion, or as a defence, of the sense which you may wish to put on it, quite apart from the question whether your interpretation itself is traditional, so it is lawful for me, though I have not the positive words of the Fathers on my side, to shelter my own interpretation of the Apostle's vision under the fact of the extant pictures of Mother and Child in the Roman Catacombs. There is another principle of Scripture interpretation which we should hold with you,—when we speak of a doctrine being contained in Scripture, we do not necessarily mean, that it is contained there in direct categorical terms, but that there is no other satisfactory way of accounting for the language and expressions of the sacred writers, concerning the subject-matter in question, than to suppose that they held upon it the opinions which we hold,—that they would not have spoken as they have spoken, *unless* they held it. For myself I have ever felt the truth of this principle, as regards the Scripture proof of the Holy Trinity; I should not have found out that doctrine in the sacred text without previous traditional teaching; but when once it is suggested from without, it commends itself as the one true interpretation, from its appositeness,—because no other view of doctrine, which can be ascribed to the inspired writers, so happily solves the obscurities and seeming inconsistencies of their teaching. And now to apply what I have said to the passage in the Apocalypse.

If there is an Apostle on whom, *à priori*, our eyes would be fixed, as likely to teach us about the Blessed Virgin, it is St. John, to whom she was committed by our Lord on the Cross,—with whom, as tradition goes, she lived at Ephesus till she was taken away. This anticipation is confirmed *à posteriori;* for, as I have said above, one of the earliest and fullest of our informants concerning her dignity, as being the second Eve, is Irenæus, who came to Lyons from Asia Minor, and had been taught by the immediate disciples of St. John. The Apostle's vision is as follows:—

"A great sign appeared in heaven: A woman clothed with the Sun, and the Moon under her feet; and on her head a crown of twelve stars. And being with child, she cried travailing in birth, and was in pain to be delivered. And there was seen another sign in heaven; and behold a great red dragon . . . And the dragon stood before the woman who was ready to be delivered, that, when she should be delivered, he might devour her son. And she brought forth a man child, who was to rule all nations with an iron rod; and her son was taken up to God and to His throne. And the woman fled into the wilderness." Now I do not deny of course, that, under the image of the Woman, the Church is signified; but what I would maintain is this, that the Holy Apostle would not have spoken of the Church under this particular image, *unless* there had existed a Blessed Virgin Mary, who was exalted on high, and the object of veneration to all the faithful.

No one doubts that the "man-child" spoken of is an allusion to our Lord: why then is not "the Woman" an allusion to His Mother? This surely is the obvious sense of the words; of course it has a further sense also, which is the scope of the image; doubtless the Child represents the children of the Church, and doubtless the Woman represents the Church; this, I grant, is the real or direct sense, but what is the sense of the symbol? *who* are the Woman and the Child? I answer, They are not personifications but Persons. This is true of the Child, therefore it is true of the Woman.

But again: not only Mother and Child, but a serpent is introduced into the vision. Such a meeting of man, woman, and serpent has not been found in Scripture, since the beginning of Scripture, and now it is found in its end. Moreover, in the passage in the Apocalypse, as if to supply, before Scripture came to an end, what was wanting in its beginning, we are told, and for the first time, that the serpent in Paradise was the evil spirit. If the dragon of St. John is the same as the serpent of Moses, and the man-child is "the seed of the woman," why is not the woman herself she, whose seed the man-child is? And, if the first woman is not an allegory, why is the second? if the first woman is Eve, why is not the second Mary?

But this is not all. The image of the woman, according to Scripture usage, is too bold and prominent for a mere personification. Scripture is not fond of allegories. We have indeed frequent figures there, as when the sacred writers speak of the arm or sword of the Lord; and so too when they speak of Jerusalem or Samaria in the feminine; or of the mountains leaping for joy, or of the Church as a bride or as a vine; but they are not much given to dressing up abstract ideas, or generalizations in personal attributes. This is the classical rather than the Scripture style. Xenophon places Hercules between Virtue and Vice, represented as women; Æschylus introduces into his drama Force and Violence; Virgil gives personality to public rumour or Fame, and Plautus to Poverty. So on monuments done in the classical style, we see virtues, vices, rivers, renown, death and the like, turned into human figures of men and women. I do not say there are no instances at all of this method in Scripture, but I say that such poetical compositions are strikingly unlike its usual method. Thus we at once feel the difference from Scripture, when we betake ourselves to the Pastor of Hermes, and find the Church a woman, to St. Methodius, and find Virtue a woman, and to St. Gregory's poem, and find Virginity again a woman. Scripture deals with types rather than personifications. Israel stands for the chosen people, David for Christ, Jerusalem for heaven. Consider the remarkable representations, dramatic I may call them, in Jeremiah, Ezechiel, and Hosea: predictions, threatenings, and promises, are acted out by those Prophets. Ezechiel is commanded to shave his head, and to divide and scatter his hair; and Ahias tears his garment, and gives ten out of twelve parts of it to Jeroboam. So too the structure of the imagery in the Apocalypse is not a mere allegorical creation, but is founded on the Jewish ritual. In like manner our Lord's bodily cures are visible types of the power of His grace upon the soul; and His prophecy of the last day is conveyed under that of the fall of Jerusalem. Even His parables are not simply ideal, but relations of occurrences, which did or might take place, under which was conveyed a spiritual meaning. The description of Wisdom in the Proverbs, and other sacred books, has brought out the instinct of commentators in this respect. They felt that Wisdom could not be a mere personification, and they determined that it was our Lord; and the later of these books, by their own more definite language, warranted that interpretation. Then, when it was found that the Arians used it in derogation of our Lord's divinity, still, unable to tolerate the notion of a mere allegory, commentators applied the description to the Blessed Virgin. Coming back then to the Apocalyptic vision, I ask, If the Woman must be some real person, who can it be whom the Apostle saw, and intends, and delineates, but that same Great Mother to whom the chapters in the Proverbs are accommodated? And let it be observed, moreover, that in this passage, from the allusion in it to the history of the fall, she may be said still to be represented under the character of the Second Eve. I make a further remark: it is sometimes asked, Why do not the sacred writers mention our Lady's greatness? I answer, she was, or may have been alive, when the Apostles and Evangelists wrote;—there was just one book of Scripture certainly written after her death, and that book does (so to say) canonize and crown her.

But if all this be so, if it is really the Blessed Virgin whom Scripture represents as clothed with the sun, crowned with the stars of heaven, and with the moon as her footstool, what height of glory may we not attribute to her? and what are we to say of those who, through ignorance, run counter to the voice of Scripture, to the testimony of the Fathers, to the traditions of East and West,

E

and speak and act contemptuously towards her whom her Lord delighteth to honour?

Now I have said all I mean to say on what I have called the rudimental teaching of Antiquity about the Blessed Virgin; but after all I have not insisted on the highest view of her prerogatives, which the Fathers have taught us. You, my dear Friend, who know so well the ancient controversies and Councils, may have been surprised why I should not have yet spoken of her as the Theotocos;—but I wished to show on how broad a basis her greatness rests, independent of that wonderful title; and again I have been loth to enlarge upon the force of a word, which is rather matter for devotional thought than for polemical dispute. However, I might as well not write on my subject at all, as altogether be silent upon it.

It is then an integral portion of the Faith fixed by Ecumenical Council, a portion of it which you hold as well as I, that the Blessed Virgin is Theotocos, Deipara, or Mother of God; and this word, when thus used, carries with it no admixture of rhetoric, no taint of extravagant affection,—it has nothing else but a well-weighed, grave, dogmatic sense, which corresponds and is adequate to its sound. It intends to express that God is her Son, as truly as any one of us is the son of his own mother. If this be so, what can be said of any creature whatever, which may not be said of her?

what can be said too much, so that it does not compromise the attributes of the Creator? He indeed might have created a being more perfect, more admirable, than she is; He might have endued that being, so created, with a richer grant of grace, of power, of blessedness: but in one respect she surpasses all even possible creations, viz. that she is Mother of her Creator. It is this awful title, which both illustrates and connects together the two prerogatives of Mary, on which I have been lately enlarging, her sanctity and her greatness. It is the issue of her sanctity; it is the source of her greatness. What dignity can be too great to attribute to her who is as closely bound up, as intimately one, with the Eternal Word, as a mother is with a son? What outfit of sanctity, what fulness and redundance of grace, what exuberance of merits must have been hers, on the supposition, which the Fathers justify, that her Maker regarded them at all, and took them into account, when he condescended "not to abhor the Virgin's womb?" Is it surprising then that on the one hand she should be immaculate in her conception? or on the other that she should be exalted as a queen with a crown of twelve stars? Men sometimes wonder that we call her Mother of life, of mercy, of salvation; what are all these titles compared to that one name, Mother of God?

I shall say no more about this title here. It is scarcely possible to write of it without diverging into a style of composition unsuited to a Letter; so I proceed to the history of its use.

The title of *Theotocos*[5] begins with ecclesiastical writers of a date hardly later than that at which we read of her as the second Eve. It first occurs in the works of Origen (185—254); but he, witnessing for Egypt and Palestine, witnesses also that it was in use before his time; for, as Socrates informs us, he "interpreted how it was to be used, and discussed the question at length" (*Hist.* vii. 32). Within two centuries (431) in the General Council held against Nestorius, it was made part of the formal dogmatic teaching of the Church. At that time, Theodoret, who from his party connexions might have been supposed disinclined to its solemn recognition, owned that "the ancient and more than ancient heralds of the orthodox faith taught the use of the term according to the Apostolic tradition." At the same date John of Antioch, who for a while sheltered Nestorius, whose heresy lay in the rejection of the term, said, "This title no ecclesiastical teacher has put aside. Those who have used it are many and eminent; and those who have not used it, have not attacked those who did." Alexander again, one of the fiercest partisans of Nestorius, witnesses to the use of the word, though he considers it dangerous; "That in festive solemnities," he says, "or in preaching or teaching, *theo-*

---
[5] Vid. Translation of St. Athanasius, pp. 420, 440, 447.

*tocos* should be unguardedly said by the orthodox without explanation is no blame, because such statements were not dogmatic, nor said with evil meaning." If we look for those, in the interval, between Origen and the Council, to whom Alexander refers, we find it used again and again by the Fathers in such of their works as are extant; by Archelaus of Mesopotamia, Eusebius of Palestine, Alexander of Egypt, in the third century; in the fourth by Athanasius many times with emphasis, by Cyril of Palestine, Gregory Nyssen of Cappadocia, Gregory Nazianzen of Cappadocia, Antiochus of Syria, and Ammonius of Thrace:—not to speak of the Emperor Julian, who, having no local or ecclesiastical domicile, speaks for the whole of Christendom. Another and earlier Emperor, Constantine, in his speech before the assembled Bishops at Nicæa, uses the still more explicit title of "the Virgin Mother of God;" which is also used by Ambrose of Milan, and by Vincent and Cassian in the south of France, and then by St. Leo.

So much for the term; it would be tedious to produce the passages of authors who, using or not using the term, convey the idea. ". Our God was carried in the womb of Mary," says Ignatius, who was martyred A.D. 106. "The word of God," says Hippolytus, "was carried in that Virgin frame." "The Maker of all," says Amphilochius, "is born of a Virgin." "She did compass without circumscribing the Sun of justice,—the Everlasting is born," says

Chrysostom. "God dwelt in the womb," says Proclus. "When thou hearest that God speaks from the bush," asks Theodotus, "in the bush seest thou not the Virgin?" Cassian says, "Mary bore her Author." "The one God only-begotten," says Hilary, "is introduced into the womb of a Virgin." "The Everlasting," says Ambrose, "came into the Virgin." "The closed gate," says Jerome, "by which alone the Lord God of Israel enters, is the Virgin Mary." "That man from heaven," says Capriolus, "is God conceived in the womb." "He is made in thee," says Augustine, "who made thee."

This being the faith of the Fathers about the Blessed Virgin, we need not wonder that it should in no long time be transmuted into devotion. No wonder if their language should become unmeasured, when so great a term as "Mother of God" had been formally set down as the safe limit of it. No wonder if it should be stronger and stronger as time went on, since only in a long period could the fulness of its import be exhausted. And in matter of fact, and as might be anticipated, (with the few exceptions which I have noted above, and which I am to treat of below,) the current of thought in those early ages did uniformly tend to make much of the Blessed Virgin and to increase her honours, not to circumscribe them. Little jealousy was shown of her in those times; but, when any such niggardness of devotion occurred, then one Father or other fell upon the offender, with zeal, not to say with fierceness. Thus St. Jerome inveighs against Helvidius; thus St. Epiphanius denounces Apollinaris, St. Cyril Nestorius, and St. Ambrose Bonosus; on the other hand, each successive insult offered to her by individual adversaries did but bring out more fully the intimate sacred affection with which Christendom regarded her. "She was alone, and wrought the world's salvation and conceived the redemption of all," says Ambrose [6]; "she had so great grace, as not only to preserve virginity herself, but to confer it upon those whom she visited." The rod out of the stem of Jesse," says Jerome, "and the Eastern gate through which the High Priest alone goes in and out, yet is ever shut." "The wise woman," says Nilus, who "hath clad believers, from the fleece of the Lamb born of her, with the clothing of incorruption, and delivered them from their spiritual nakedness." "The mother of life, of beauty, of majesty, the morning star," according to Antiochus. "The mystical new heavens," "the heavens carrying the Divinity," "the fruitful vine," "by whom we are translated from death to life," according to St. Ephrem. "The manna, which is delicate, bright, sweet, and virgin, which, as though coming from heaven, has poured down on all the people of the Churches a food pleasanter than honey," according to St. Maximus.

[6] Essay on Doctr. Dev. p. 408.

Basil of Seleucia says, that "she shines out above all the martyrs as the sun above the stars, and that she mediates between God and men." "Run through all creation in your thought," says Proclus, "and see if there be one equal or superior to the Holy Virgin, Mother of God." "Hail, Mother, clad in light, of the light which sets not;" says Theodotus, or some one else at Ephesus, "hail, all-undefiled mother of holiness; hail, most pellucid fountain of the life-giving stream." And St. Cyril too at Ephesus, "Hail, Mary Mother of God, majestic common-treasure of the whole world, the lamp unquenchable, the crown of virginity, the sceptre of orthodoxy, the indissoluble temple, the dwelling of the Illimitable, Mother and Virgin, through whom He in the holy gospels is called blessed who cometh in the name of the Lord, .... through whom the Holy Trinity is sanctified, ..... through whom Angels and Archangels rejoice, devils are put to flight, .... and the fallen creature is received up into the heavens, &c., &c.'." Such is but a portion of the panegyrical language which St. Cyril used in the third Ecumenical Council.

I must not close my review of the Catholic doctrine concerning the Blessed Virgin, without directly speaking of her intercessory power, though I have incidentally made mention of it already. It

---

' Opp. t. 6, p. 355.

is the immediate result of two truths, neither of which you dispute;—first, that "it is good and useful," as the Council of Trent says, "suppliantly to invoke the saints and to have recourse to their prayers;" and secondly, that the Blessed Mary is singularly dear to her Son and singularly exalted in sanctity and glory. However, at the risk of becoming didactic, I will state somewhat more fully the grounds on which it rests.

To a candid pagan, it must have been one of the most remarkable points of Christianity, on its first appearance, that the observance of prayer formed so vital a part of its organization; and that, though its members were scattered all over the world, and its rulers and subjects had so little opportunity of correlative action, yet they, one and all, found the solace of a spiritual intercourse and a real bond of union, in the practice of mutual intercession. Prayer indeed is the very essence of religion; but in the heathen religions it was either public or personal; it was a state ordinance, or a selfish expedient, for the attainment of certain tangible, temporal goods. Very different from this was its exercise among Christians, who were thereby knit together in one body, different, as they were, in races, ranks, and habits, distant from each other in country, and helpless amid hostile populations. Yet it proved sufficient for its purpose. Christians could not correspond; they could not combine; but they could pray one for another. Even their public prayers partook of this character of intercession; for to pray for the welfare of the whole Church was in fact a prayer for all the classes of men, and all the individuals of which it was composed. It was in prayer that the Church was founded. For ten days all the Apostles "persevered with one mind in prayer and supplication, with the women, and Mary the Mother of Jesus, and with His brethren." Then again at Pentecost "they were all with one mind in one place;" and the converts then made are said to have "persevered in prayer." And when, after a while, St. Peter was seized and put in prison with a view to his being put to death, "prayer was made without ceasing" by the Church of God for him; and, when the angel released him, he took refuge in a house "where many were gathered together in prayer."

We are so accustomed to these passages, as hardly to be able to do justice to their singular significance; and they are followed up by various passages of the Apostolic Epistles. St. Paul enjoins his brethren to "pray with all prayer and supplication at all times in the Spirit, with all instance and supplication for all saints," to "pray in every place," "to make supplication, prayers, intercessions, giving of thanks, for all men." And in his own person he "ceases not to give thanks for them, commemorating them in his prayers," and "always in all his prayers making supplication for them all with joy."

Now, was this spiritual bond to cease with life?

or had Christians similar duties to their brethren departed? From the witness of the early ages of the Church, it appears that they had; and you, and those who agree with you, would be the last to deny that they were then in the practice of praying, as for the living, so for those also who had passed into the intermediate state between earth and heaven. Did the sacred communion extend further still, on to the inhabitants of heaven itself? Here too you agree with us, for you have adopted in your Volume the words of the Council of Trent, which I have quoted above. But now we are brought to a higher order of thought.

It would be preposterous to pray for those who are already in glory; but at least they can pray for us, and we can ask their prayers, and in the Apocalypse at least Angels are introduced both sending us their blessing and presenting our prayers before the Divine Presence. We read there of an Angel who "came and stood before the altar, having a golden censer;" and "there was given to him much incense, that he should offer of the prayers of all saints upon the golden altar which is before the Throne of God." On this occasion, surely the Angel (Michael, as the prayer in Mass considers him), performed the part of a great Intercessor or Mediator above for the children of the Church Militant below. Again, in the beginning of the same book, the sacred writer goes so far as to speak of "grace and peace" coming to us, not only from the Almighty, but "from the seven Spirits that are before His throne," thus associating the Eternal with the ministers of His mercies; and this carries us on to the remarkable passage of St. Justin, one of the earliest Fathers, who, in his Apology, says, "To Him (God), and His Son who came from Him and taught us these things, and the host of the other good Angels who follow and resemble Him, and the Prophetic Spirit, we pay veneration and homage." Further, in the Epistle to the Hebrews, St. Paul introduces, not only Angels, but "the spirits of the just" into the sacred communion: "Ye have come to Mount Sion, to the heavenly Jerusalem, to myriads of angels, to God the Judge of all, to the spirits of the just made perfect, and to Jesus the Mediator of the New Testament." What can be meant by having "come to the spirits of the just," unless in some way or other they do us good, whether by blessing or by aiding us? that is, in a word, to speak correctly, by praying for us, for it is by prayer alone that the creature above can bless or aid the creature below.

Intercession thus being a first principle of the Church's life, next it is certain again, that the vital principle of that intercession, as an availing power, is, according to the will of God, sanctity. This seems to be suggested by a passage of St. Paul, in which the Supreme Intercessor is said to be "the Spirit:"—"the Spirit Himself maketh intercession for us; He maketh intercession for the saints according to God." However, the truth thus implied, is expressly brought out in other parts of Scripture, in the form both of doctrine and of example. The words of the man born blind speak the common-sense of nature:—" if any man be a worshipper of God, him He heareth." And Apostles confirm them:—" the prayer of a just man availeth much," and "whatever we ask, we receive, because we keep his commandments." Then, as for examples, we read of Abraham and Moses, as having the divine purpose of judgment revealed to them beforehand, in order that they might deprecate its execution. To the friends of Job it was said, "My servant Job shall pray for you; his face I will accept." Elias by his prayer shut and opened the heavens. Elsewhere we read of "Jeremias, Moses, and Samuel;" and of "Noe, Daniel, and Job," as being great mediators between God and His people. One instance is given us, which testifies the continuance of so high an office beyond this life. Lazarus, in the parable, is seen in Abraham's bosom. It is usual to pass over this striking passage with the remark that it is a Jewish expression; whereas, Jewish belief or not, it is recognized and sanctioned by our Lord Himself. What do we teach about the Blessed Virgin more wonderful than this? Let us suppose, that, at the hour of death, the faithful are committed to her arms; but if Abraham, not yet ascended on high, had charge of Lazarus, what offence is it to affirm the like of her, who was not merely "the friend," but the very "Mother of God?"

It may be added, that, though it availed nothing for influence with our Lord, to be one of His company, if sanctity was wanting, still, as the Gospel shows, He on various occasions allowed those who were near Him, to be the means by which supplicants were brought to Him or miracles gained from Him, as in the instance of the miracle of the loaves; and if on one occasion, He seems to repel His Mother, when she told Him that wine was wanting for the guests at the marriage feast, it is obvious to remark on it, that, by saying that she was then separated from Him, *because* His hour was not yet come, He implied, that when that hour was come, such separation would be at an end. Moreover, in fact He did, at her intercession, work the miracle which she desired.

I consider it impossible then, for those who believe the Church to be one vast body in heaven and on earth, in which every holy creature of God has his place, and of which prayer is the life, when once they recognize the sanctity and greatness of the Blessed Virgin, not to perceive immediately, that her office above is one of perpetual intercession for the faithful militant, and that our very relation to her must be that of clients to a patron, and that, in the eternal enmity which exists between the woman and the serpent, while the serpent's strength is that of being the Tempter, the weapon of the Second Eve and Mother of God is prayer.

As then these ideas of her sanctity and greatness gradually penetrated the mind of Christendom, so did that of her intercessory power follow close upon them and with them. From the earliest times that mediation is symbolized in those representations of her with up-lifted hands, which, whether in plaster or in glass, are still extant in Rome,—that Church, as St. Irenæus says, with which "every Church, that is, the faithful from every side, must agree, because of its more powerful principality;" "into which," as Tertullian adds, "the Apostles poured out, together with their blood, their whole doctrines." As far indeed as existing documents are concerned, I know of no instance to my purpose earlier than A.D. 234, but it is a very remarkable one; and, though it has been often quoted in the controversy, an argument is not the weaker for frequent use.

St. Gregory Nyssen[a], then, a native of Cappadocia in the fourth century, relates that his name-sake, Bishop of Neo-Cæsarea, surnamed Thaumaturgus, in the century preceding, shortly before he was called to the priesthood, received in a vision a Creed, which is still extant, from the Blessed Mary at the hands of St. John. The account runs thus:—He was deeply pondering theological doctrine, which

[a] Vid. Essay on Doctr. Dev. p. 386.

the heretics of the day depraved. "In such thoughts," says his name-sake of Nyssa, " he was passing the night, when one appeared, as if in human form, aged in appearance, saintly in the fashion of his garments, and very venerable both in grace of countenance and general mien. Amazed at the sight, he started from his bed, and asked who it was, and why he came; but, on the other calming the perturbation of his mind with his gentle voice, and saying he had appeared to him by divine command on account of his doubts, in order that the truth of the orthodox faith might be revealed to him, he took courage at the word, and regarded him with a mixture of joy and fright. Then, on his stretching his hand straight forward and pointing with his fingers at something on one side, he followed with his eyes the extended hand, and saw another appearance opposite to the former, in shape of a woman, but more than human. . . . When his eyes could not bear the apparition, he heard them conversing together on the subject of his doubts; and thereby not only gained a true knowledge of the faith, but learned their names, as they addressed each other by their respective appellations. And thus he is said to have heard the person in woman's shape bid 'John the Evangelist' disclose to the young man the mystery of godliness; and he answered that he was ready to comply in this matter with the wish of 'the Mother of the Lord,' and enunciated a formulary, well-turned and complete, and so vanished. He, on the other hand, immediately committed to writing that divine teaching of his mystagogue, and henceforth preached in the Church according to that form, and bequeathed to posterity, as an inheritance, that heavenly teaching, by means of which his people are instructed down to this day, being preserved from all heretical evil." He proceeds to rehearse the Creed thus given, "There is One God, Father of a Living Word," &c. Bull, after quoting it in his work upon the Nicene Faith, alludes to this history of its origin, and adds, "No one should think it incredible that such a providence should befall a man whose whole life was conspicuous for revelations and miracles, as all ecclesiastical writers who have mentioned him (and who has not?) witness with one voice."

Here she is represented as rescuing a holy soul from intellectual error. This leads me to a further reflection. You seem, in one place in your Volume, to object to the Antiphon, in which it is said of her, "All heresies thou hast destroyed alone." Surely the truth of it is verified in this age, as in former times, and especially by the doctrine concerning her, on which I have been dwelling. She is the great exemplar of prayer in a generation, which emphatically denies the power of prayer *in toto*, which determines that fatal laws govern the universe, that there cannot be any direct communication between earth and heaven, that God

F

cannot visit His earth, and that man cannot influence His providence.

I cannot help hoping that your own reading of the Fathers will on the whole bear me out in the above account of their teaching concerning the Blessed Virgin. Anglicans seem to me to overlook the strength of the argument adducible from their works in our favour, and they open the attack upon our mediæval and modern writers, careless of leaving a host of primitive opponents in their rear. I do not include you among such Anglicans, as you know what the Fathers assert; but, if so, have you not, my dear Friend, been unjust to yourself in your recent Volume, and made far too much of the differences which exist between Anglicans and us on this particular point? It is the office of an Irenicon to smoothe difficulties; I shall be pleased if I succeed in removing some of yours. Let the public judge between us here. Had you happened in your Volume to introduce your notice of our teaching about the Blessed Virgin, with a notice of the teaching of the Fathers concerning her, ordinary men would have considered that there was not much to choose between you and us. Though you appealed ever so much, in your defence, to the authority of the " undivided Church," they would have said that you, who had such high notions of the Blessed Mary, were one of the last men who had a right to accuse us of quasi-idolatry. When they found you calling her by the titles of Mother of God, Second Eve, and Mother of all Living, the Mother of Life, the Morning Star, the mystical new heaven, the sceptre of Orthodoxy, the All-undefiled Mother of Holiness, and the like, they would have deemed it a poor compensation for such language, that you protested against her being called a Co-redemptress or a Priestess.  And, if they were violent Protestants, they would not have read you with that relish and gratitude with which, as it is, they have perhaps accepted your testimony against us.  Not that they would have been altogether right in their view of you;—on the contrary I think there is a real difference between what you protest against, and what with the Fathers you hold; but unread men and men of the world form a broad practical judgment of the things which come before them, and they would have felt in this case that they had the same right to be shocked at you, as you have to be shocked at us;—and further, which is the point to which I am coming, they would have said, that, granting some of our modern writers go beyond the Fathers in this matter, still the line cannot be logically drawn between the teaching of the Fathers concerning the Blessed Virgin and our own.  This view of the matter seems to me true and important; I do not think the line *can* be satisfactorily drawn, and to this point I shall now direct my attention.

It is impossible, I say, in a doctrine like this, to draw the line cleanly between truth and error, right and wrong. This is ever the case in concrete matters, which have life. Life in this world is motion, and involves a continual process of change. Living things grow into their perfection, into their decline, into their death. No rule of art will suffice to stop the operation of this natural law, whether in the material world or in the human mind. We can indeed encounter disorders, when they occur, by external antagonisms and remedies; but we cannot eradicate the process itself, out of which they arise. Life has the same right to decay, as it has to wax strong. This is specially the case with great ideas. You may stifle them; or you may refuse them elbow-room; or you may torment them with your continual meddling; or you may let them have free course and range, and be content, instead of anticipating their excesses, to expose and restrain those excesses after they have occurred. But you have only this alternative; and for myself, I prefer much, wherever it is possible, to be first generous and then just; to grant full liberty of thought, and to call it to account when abused.

If what I have been saying be true of energetic ideas generally, much more is it the case in matters of religion. Religion acts on the affections; who is to hinder these, when once roused, from gathering in their strength and running wild? They are not gifted with any connatural principle within them, which renders them self-governing and self-adjusting. They hurry right on to their object, and often in their case it is, The more haste, the worse speed. Their object engrosses them, and they see nothing else. And of all passions love is the most unmanageable; nay more, I would not give much for that love which is never extravagant, which always observes the proprieties, and can move about in perfect good taste, under all emergencies. What mother, what husband or wife, what youth or maiden in love, but says a thousand foolish things, in the way of endearment, which the speaker would be sorry for strangers to hear; yet they are not on that account unwelcome to the parties to whom they are addressed. Sometimes by bad luck they are written down, sometimes they get into the newspapers; and what might be even graceful, when it was fresh from the heart, and interpreted by the voice and the countenance, presents but a melancholy exhibition when served up cold for the public eye. So it is with devotional feelings. Burning thoughts and words are as open to criticism as they are beyond it. What is abstractedly extravagant, may in religious persons be becoming and beautiful, and only fall under blame when it is found in others who imitate them. When it is formalized into meditations or exercises, it is as repulsive as love-letters in a police report. Moreover, even holy minds readily adopt and become familiar with language which they would never have originated themselves, when it proceeds from a writer who has the same objects of devotion as they have; and, if they find a stranger ridicule or reprobate supplication or praise which has come to them so recommended, they feel it as keenly as if a direct insult were offered to those to whom that homage is addressed. In the next place, what has power to stir holy and refined souls is potent also with the multitude; and the religion of the multitude is ever vulgar and abnormal; it ever will be tinctured with fanaticism and superstition, while men are what they are. A people's religion is ever a corrupt religion, in spite of the provisions of Holy Church. If she is to be Catholic, you must put up with fish of every kind, guests good and bad, vessels of gold, vessels of earth. You may beat religion out of men, if you will, and then their excesses will take a different direction; but if you make use of religion to improve them, they will make use of religion to corrupt it. And then you will have effected that compromise of which our countrymen report so unfavourably from abroad:— a high grand faith and worship which compels their admiration, and puerile absurdities among the people which excite their contempt.

Nor is it any safeguard against these excesses in a religious system, that the religion is based upon reason, and developes into a theology. Theology both uses logic and baffles it; and thus logic acts both as a protection and as the perversion of religion. Theology is occupied with supernatural matters, and is ever running into mysteries, which reason can neither explain nor adjust. Its lines of thought come to an abrupt termination, and to pursue them or to complete them is to plunge down the abyss. But logic blunders on, forcing its way, as it can, through thick darkness and ethereal mediums. The Arians went ahead with logic for their directing principle, and so lost the truth; on the other hand, St. Augustine, in his Treatise on the Holy Trinity, seems to show that, if we attempt to find and tie together the ends of lines which run into infinity, we shall only succeed in contradicting ourselves; that for instance it is difficult to find the logical reason for not speaking of three Gods as well as of One, and of One Person in the Godhead as well as of Three. I do not mean to say that logic cannot be used to set right its own error, or that in the hands of an able disputant the balance of truth may not be restored. This was done at the Councils of Antioch and Nicæa, in the instances of Paulus and Arius. But such a process is circuitous and elaborate; and is conducted by means of minute subtleties which will give it the appearance of a game of skill in the case of matters too grave and practical to deserve a mere scholastic treatment. Accordingly St. Augustine simply lays it down that the statements in question are heretical, for the former is Tritheism and the latter Sabellianism. That is, good sense and a large view of truth, are the correctives of his logic. And thus we have arrived at the final resolution of the whole matter; for good sense and a large view of truth are rare gifts; whereas all men are bound to be devout, and most men think they can argue and conclude.

Now let me apply what I have been saying to the teaching of the Church on the subject of the Blessed Virgin. I have to recur to a subject of so sacred a nature, that, writing as I am for publication, I need the apology of my object for venturing to pursue it. I say then, when once we have mastered the idea, that Mary bore, suckled, and handled the Eternal in the form of a child, what limit is conceivable to the rush and flood of thoughts which such a doctrine involves? What awe and surprise must attend upon the knowledge, that a creature has been brought so close to the Divine Essence? It was the creation of a new idea and of a new sympathy, of a new faith and worship, when the holy Apostles announced that God had become incarnate; and a supreme love and devotion to Him became possible, which seemed hopeless before that revelation. But besides this, a second range of thoughts was opened on mankind, unknown before, and unlike any other, as soon as it was understood that that Incarnate God had a mother. The second idea is perfectly distinct from the former, the one does not interfere with the other. He is God made low, she is a woman made high. I scarcely like to use a familiar illustration

on such a subject, but it will serve to explain what
I mean, when I ask you to consider the difference of
feeling, with which we read the respective histories
of Maria Theresa and the Maid of Orleans; or with
which the middle and lower classes of a nation
regard a first minister of the day who has come of
an aristocratic house, and one who has risen from
the ranks. May God's mercy keep me from the
shadow of a thought dimming the purity or blunting
the keenness of that love of Him, which is our sole
happiness and our sole salvation! But surely
when He became man, He brought home to us His
incommunicable attributes with a distinctiveness,
which precludes the possibility of our lowering Him
merely by exalting a creature. He alone has an
entrance into our soul, reads our secret thoughts,
speaks to our heart, applies to us spiritual pardon
and strength. On Him we solely depend. He
alone is our inward life; He not only regenerates
us, but (to allude to a higher mystery) *semper
gignit;* He is ever renewing our new birth and
our heavenly sonship. In this sense He may be
called, as in nature, so in grace, our real Father.
Mary is only our mother by adoption, given us from
the Cross; her presence is above, not on earth;
her office is external, not within us. Her name is
not heard in the administration of the Sacraments.
Her work is not one of ministration towards us;
her power is indirect. It is her prayers that avail,
and they are effectual by the *fiat* of Him who is

our all in all. Nor need she hear us by any innate power, or any personal gift; but by His manifestation to her of the prayers which we make her. When Moses was on the Mount, the Almighty told him of the idolatry of his people at the foot of it, in order that he might intercede for them; and thus it is the Divine Presence which is the intermediating Power by which we reach her and she reaches us.

Woe is me, if even by a breath I sully these ineffable truths! but still, without prejudice to them, there is, I say, another range of thought quite distinct from them, incommensurate with them, of which the Blessed Virgin is the centre. If we placed our Lord in that centre, we should only be degrading Him from His throne, and making Him an Arian kind of a God; that is, no God at all. He who charges us with making Mary a divinity, is thereby denying the divinity of Jesus. Such a man does not know what divinity is. Our Lord cannot pray for us, as a creature, as Mary prays; He cannot inspire those feelings which a creature inspires. To her belongs, as being a creature, a natural claim on our sympathy and familiarity, in that she is nothing else than our fellow. She is our pride,—in the poet's words, "Our tainted nature's solitary boast." We look to her without any fear, any remorse, any consciousness that she is able to read us, judge us, punish us. Our heart yearns towards that pure Virgin, that gentle Mother, and our congratulations follow

her, as she rises from Nazareth and Ephesus,
through the choirs of angels, to her throne on high.
So weak yet so strong; so delicate, yet so glory-
laden; so modest, yet so mighty. She has sketched
for us her own portrait in the Magnificat. "He
hath regarded the low estate of His hand-maid; for
behold, from henceforth all generations shall call
me blessed. He hath put down the mighty from
their seat; and hath exalted the humble. He hath
filled the hungry with good things, and the rich He
hath sent empty away." I recollect the strange
emotion which took by surprise men and women,
young and old, when, at the Coronation of our
present Queen, they gazed on the figure of one so
like a child, so small, so tender, so shrinking, who
had been exalted to so great an inheritance and so
vast a rule, who was such a contrast in her own
person to the solemn pageant which centred in her.
Could it be otherwise with the spectators, if they
had human affection? And did not the All-wise
know the human heart when He took to Himself a
Mother? did He not anticipate our emotion at the
sight of such an exaltation? If He had not meant
her to exert that wonderful influence in His Church,
which she has in the event exerted, I will use a bold
word, He it is who has perverted us. If she is not
to attract our homage, why did He make her solitary in her greatness amid His vast creation? If
it be idolatry in us to let our affections respond to
our faith, He would not have made her what she

is; or He would not have told us that He had so made her; but, far from this, He has sent His Prophet to announce to us, "A Virgin shall conceive and bear a Son, and they shall call His name Emmanuel," and we have the same warrant for hailing her as God's Mother, as we have for adoring Him as God.

Christianity is eminently an objective religion. For the most part it tells us of persons and facts in simple words, and leaves the announcement to produce its effect on such hearts as are prepared to receive it. This at least is its general character; and Butler recognizes it as such in his Analogy, when speaking of the Second and Third Persons of the Holy Trinity:—"The internal worship," he says, "to the Son and Holy Ghost is no farther matter of pure revealed command than as the relations they stand in to us are matters of pure revelation; for the relations being known, the obligations to such internal worship are *obligations of reason arising out of those relations themselves*[\*]." It is in this way that the revealed doctrine of the Incarnation exerted a stronger and a broader influence on Christians, as they more and more apprehended and mastered its meaning and its bearings. It is contained in the brief and simple declaration of St. John, "The Word was made flesh;" but it required century after century to spread it out in its fulness, and to im-

---

[\*] Vid. Essay on Doctr. Dev., p. 50.

print it energetically on the worship and practice of the Catholic people as well as on their faith. Athanasius was the first and the great teacher of it. He collected together the inspired notices scattered through David, Isaias, St. Paul, and St. John, and he engraved indelibly upon the imaginations of the faithful, as had never been before, that man is God, and God is man, that in Mary they meet, and that in this sense Mary is the centre of all things. He added nothing to what was known before, nothing to the popular and zealous faith that her Son was God; he has left behind him in his works no such definite passages about her as those of St. Irenæus or St. Epiphanius; but he brought the circumstances of the Incarnation home to men's minds, by the manifold evolutions of his analysis, and secured it for ever from perversion. Still, however, there was much to be done; we have no proof that Athanasius himself had any special devotion to the Blessed Virgin; but he laid the foundations on which that devotion was to rest, and thus noiselessly and without strife, as the first Temple in the Holy City, she grew up into her inheritance, and was "established in Sion and her power was in Jerusalem." Such was the origin of that august *cultus* which has been paid to the Blessed Mary for so many centuries in the East and in the West. That in times and places it has fallen into abuse, that it has even become a superstition, I do not care to deny; for, as I have said above, the same process which brings to maturity carries on to decay, and things that do not admit of abuse have very little life in them. This of course does not excuse such excesses, or justify us in making light of them, when they occur. I have no intention of doing so as regards the particular instances which you bring against us, though but a few words will suffice for what I need say about them:—before doing so, however, I am obliged to make three or four introductory remarks.

1. I have almost anticipated my first remark already. It is this: that the height of our offending in our devotion to the Blessed Virgin would not look so great in your Volume as it does, had you not placed yourself on lower ground than your own feelings towards her would have spontaneously prompted you to take. I have no doubt you had some good reason for adopting this course, but I do not know it; what I do know is, that, for the Fathers' sake who so exalt her, you really do love and venerate her, though you do not evidence it in your book. I am glad then in this place to insist on a fact which will lead those among us, who know you not, to love you from their love of her, in spite of what you refuse to give her; and Anglicans, on the other hand, who do know you, to think better of us, who refuse her nothing, when they reflect that you do not actually go against us, but merely come short of us, in your devotion to her.

2. As you revere the Fathers, so you revere the Greek Church; and here again we have a witness on our behalf, of which you must be aware as fully as we are, and of which you must really mean to give us the benefit. In proportion as this remarkable fact is understood, it will take off the edge of the surprise of Anglicans at the sight of our devotions to our Lady. It must weigh with them, when they discover that we can enlist on our side in this controversy those "seventy millions" (I think they so consider them) of Orientals, who are separated from our communion. Is it not a very pregnant fact, that the Eastern Churches, so independent of us, so long separated from the West, so jealous of Antiquity, should even surpass us in their exaltation of the Blessed Virgin? That they go further than we do is sometimes denied, on the ground that the Western devotion towards her is brought out into system, and the Eastern is not; yet this only means really, that the Latins have more mental activity, more strength of intellect, less of routine, less of mechanical worship among them, than the Greeks. We are able, better than they, to give an account of what we do; and we seem to be more extreme, merely because we are more definite. But, after all, what have the Latins done so bold, as that substitution of the name of Mary for the Name of Jesus at the end of the collects and petitions in the Breviary, nay in the Ritual and Liturgy? Not merely in local or popu-

lar, and in semi-authorized devotions, which are the kind of sources that supplies you with your matter of accusation against us, but in the formal prayers of the Greek Eucharistic Service, petitions are offered, not "in the name of Jesus Christ," but "of the Theotocos." Such a phenomenon, in such a quarter, I think ought to make Anglicans merciful towards those writers among ourselves, who have been excessive in singing the praises of the Deipara. To make a rule of substituting Mary with all Saints for Jesus in the public service, has more "Mariolatry" in it, than to alter the Te Deum to her honour in private devotion.

3. And thus I am brought to a third remark, supplemental to your accusation of us. Two large views, as I have said above, are opened upon our devotional thoughts in Christianity; the one centering in the Son of Mary, the other in the Mother of Jesus. Neither need obscure the other; and in the Catholic Church, as a matter of fact, neither does. I wish you had either frankly allowed this in your Volume, or proved the contrary. I wish, when you report that "a certain proportion, it has been ascertained by those who have inquired, do stop short in her," p. 107, that you had added your belief, that the case was far otherwise with the great bulk of Catholics. Might I not have expected it? May I not, without sensitiveness, be somewhat pained at the omission? From mere Protestants indeed I expect nothing better. They con-

tent themselves with saying that our devotions to our Lady *must necessarily* throw our Lord into the shade; and thereby they relieve themselves of a great deal of trouble. Then they catch at any stray fact which countenances or seems to countenance their prejudice. Now I say plainly I never will defend or screen any one from your just rebuke, who, through false devotion to Mary, forgets Jesus. But I should like the fact to be proved first; I cannot hastily admit it. There is this broad fact the other way;—that, if we look through Europe, we shall find, on the whole, that just those nations and countries have lost their faith in the divinity of Christ, who have given up devotion to His Mother, and that those on the other hand, who have been foremost in her honour, have retained their orthodoxy. Contrast, for instance, the Calvinists with the Greeks, or France with the North of Germany, or the Protestant and Catholic communions in Ireland. As to England, it is scarcely doubtful what would be the state of its Established Church, if the Liturgy and Articles were not an integral part of its Establishment; and, when men bring so grave a charge against us as is implied in your Volume, they cannot be surprised if we in turn say hard things of Anglicanism[1]. In the Catholic Church Mary has

[1] I have spoken more on this subject in my Essay on Development, p. 438, "Nor does it avail to object, that, in this contrast of devotional exercises, the human is sure to supplant the

G

shown herself, not the rival, but the minister of her Son; she has protected Him, as in His infancy, so in the whole history of the Religion. There is then a plain historical truth in Dr. Faber's words which you quote to condemn, " Jesus is obscured, because Mary is kept in the back-ground."

This truth, exemplified in history, might also be abundantly illustrated, did my space admit, from the lives and writings of holy men in modern times. Two of them, St. Alfonso Liguori and the Blessed Paul of the Cross, for all their notorious devotion to the Mother, have shown their supreme love of her Divine Son, in the names which they have given to their respective congregations, viz. " of the Redeemer," and " of the Cross and Passion." However, I will do no more than refer to an apposite passage in the Italian translation of the work of a French Jesuit, Fr. Nepveu, " Christian Thoughts

Divine, from the infirmity of our nature; for, I repeat, the question is one of fact, whether it has done so. And next, it must be asked, *whether the character of Protestant devotion towards our Lord, has been that of worship at all;* and not rather such as we pay to an excellent human being. . . . Carnal minds will ever create a carnal worship for themselves; and to forbid them the service of the saints will have no tendency to teach them the worship of God. Moreover, . . . great and constant as is the devotion which the Catholic pays to St. Mary, it has a special province, and *has far more connexion with the public services and the festive aspect of Christianity,* and with certain extraordinary offices which she holds, *than with what is strictly personal and primary* in religion." Our late Cardinal, on my reception, singled out to me this last sentence, for the expression of his especial approbation.

for every Day in the Year," which was recommended to the friend who went with me to Rome, by the same Jesuit Father there, with whom, as I have already said, I stood myself in such intimate relations; I believe it is a fair specimen of the teaching of our spiritual books.

"The love of Jesus Christ is the most sure pledge of our future happiness, and the most infallible token of our predestination. Mercy towards the poor, devotion to the Holy Virgin, are very sensible tokens of predestination; nevertheless they are not absolutely infallible; but one cannot have a sincere and constant love of Jesus Christ, without being predestinated. . . . The destroying angel, which bereaved the houses of the Egyptians of their first-born, had respect to all the houses which were marked with the blood of the Lamb."

And it is also exemplified, as I verily believe, not only in formal and distinctive Confessions, not only in books intended for the educated class, but also in the personal religion of the Catholic populations. When strangers are so unfavourably impressed with us, because they see Images of our Lady in our Churches, and crowds flocking about her, they forget that there is a Presence within the sacred walls, infinitely more awful, which claims and obtains from us a worship transcendently different from any devotion we pay to her. That devotion might indeed tend to idolatry, if it were encouraged in Protestant Churches, where there is nothing higher than it to attract the worshipper; but all the images that a Catholic Church ever contained, all the Crucifixes at its Altars brought together, do not so affect its frequenters, as the lamp which betokens the presence or absence there of the Blessed Sacrament. Is not this so certain, so notorious, that on some occasions it has been even brought as a charge against us, that we are irreverent in Church, when what seemed to the objector to be irreverence was but the necessary change of feeling, which came over those who were there, on their knowing that their Lord was away?

The Mass again conveys to us the same lesson of the sovereignty of the Incarnate Son; it is a return to Calvary, and Mary is scarcely named in it. Hostile visitors enter our Churches on Sunday at midday, the time of the Anglican Service. They are surprised to see the High Mass perhaps poorly attended, and a body of worshippers leaving the music and the mixed multitude who may be lazily fulfilling their obligation, for the silent or the informal devotions which are offered at an Image of the Blessed Virgin. They may be tempted, with one of your informants, to call such a temple, not a "Jesus Church," but a "Mary Church." But, if they understood our ways, they would know that we begin the day with our Lord and then go on to His Mother. It is early in the morning that religious persons go to Mass and Communion. The High Mass, on the other hand, is the festive celebration of the day, not the special devotional service; nor is there any reason why those who have been at a Low Mass already, should not at that hour proceed to ask the intercession of the Blessed Virgin for themselves and all that is dear to them.

Communion, again, which is given in the morning, is a solemn unequivocal act of faith in the Incarnate God, if any can be such; and the most gracious of admonitions, did we need one, of His sovereign and sole right to possess us. I knew a lady, who on her death-bed was visited by an excellent Protestant friend. She, with great tenderness for her soul's welfare, asked her whether her prayers to the Blessed Virgin did not, at that awful hour, lead to forgetfulness of her Saviour. "Forget Him?" she replied with surprise, "Why, He has just been here." She had been receiving Him in communion. When then, my dear Pusey, you read any thing extravagant in praise of our Lady, is it not charitable to ask, even while you condemn it in itself, did the author write nothing else? Did he write on the Blessed Sacrament? had he given up "all for Jesus?" I recollect some lines, the happiest, I think, which that author wrote, which bring out strikingly the reciprocity, which I am dwelling on, of the respective devotions to Mother and Son;

> "But scornful men have coldly said
>     Thy love was leading me from God;
> And yet in this I did but tread
>     The very path my Saviour trod.
>
> "They know but little of thy worth
>     Who speak these heartless words to me;
> For what did Jesus love on earth
>     One half so tenderly as thee?

"Get me the grace to love thee more;
   Jesus will give, if thou wilt plead;
And, Mother, when life's cares are o'er,
   Oh, I shall love thee then indeed.

"Jesus, when His three hours were run,
   Bequeathed thee from the Cross to me;
And oh! how can I love thy Son,
   Sweet Mother, if I love not thee.".

4. Thus we are brought from the consideration of the sentiments themselves, of which you complain, to the persons who wrote, and the places where they wrote them. I wish you had been led, in this part of your work, to that sort of careful labour which you have employed in so masterly a way in your investigation of the circumstances of the definition of the Immaculate Conception. In the latter case you have catalogued the Bishops who wrote to the Holy See, and analyzed their answers. Had you in like manner discriminated and located the Marian writers, as you call them, and observed the times, places, and circumstances of their works, I think, they would not, when brought together, have had their present startling effect on the reader. As it is, they inflict a vague alarm upon the mind, as when one hears a noise, and does not know whence it comes and what it means. Some of your authors, I know are Saints; all, I suppose, are spiritual writers and holy men; but the majority are of no great celebrity, even if they have any kind of weight. Suarez has no business among them at all, for, when he says that no one is saved without the Blessed Virgin, he is speak-

ing not of devotion to her, but of her intercession. The greatest name is St. Alfonso Liguori; but it never surprises me to read any thing unusual in the devotions of a saint. Such men are on a level very different from our own, and we cannot understand them. I hold this to be an important canon in the Lives of the Saints, according to the words of the Apostle, "The spiritual man judges all . things, and he himself is judged of no one." But we may refrain from judging, without proceeding to imitate. I hope it is not disrespectful to so great a servant of God to say, that I never have read his Glories of Mary; but here I am speaking generally of all Saints, whether I know them or not; —and I say that they are beyond us, and that we must use them as patterns, not as copies. As to his practical directions, St. Alfonso wrote them for Neapolitans, whom he knew, and we do not know. Other writers whom you quote, as de Salazar, are too ruthlessly logical to be safe or pleasant guides in the delicate matters of devotion. As to de Montford and Oswald, I never even met with their names, till I saw them in your book; the bulk of our laity, not to say of our clergy, perhaps know them little better than I do. Nor did I know till I learnt it from your Volume, that there were two Bernardines. St. Bernardine of Sienna, I knew of course, and knew too that he had a burning love for our Lord. But about the other, "Bernardine de Bustis," I was quite at fault. I find from the Protestant Cave, that he, as well as his namesake, made himself conspicuous also for his zeal for the Holy Name, which is much to the point here. "With such devotion was he carried away," says Cave, "for the bare name of Jesus, (which, by a new device of Bernardine of Sienna, had lately begun to receive divine honours,) that he was urgent with Innocent VIII. to assign it a day and rite in the Calendar."

One thing, however, is clear about all these writers; that not one of them is an Englishman. I have gone through your book, and do not find one English name among the various authors to whom you refer, except of course the name of that author whose lines I have been quoting, and who, great as are his merits, cannot, for the reasons I have given in the opening of my Letter, be considered a representative of English Catholic devotion. Whatever these writers may have said or not said, whatever they may have said harshly, and whatever capable of fair explanation, still they are foreigners; we are not answerable for their particular devotions; and as to themselves, I am glad to be able to quote the beautiful words which you use about them in your letter to the Weekly Register of November 25th last. "I do not presume," you say, "to prescribe to Italians or Spaniards, what they shall hold, or how they shall express their pious opinions; and least of all did I think of imputing to any of the writers whom I quoted that they took from our Lord any of the love which they gave to His Mother." In these last words too you have supplied one of the omissions in your Volume which I noticed above.

5. Now then we come to England itself, which after all, in the matter of devotion, alone concerns you and me; for though doctrine is one and the same every where, devotions, as I have already said, are matters of the particular time and the particular country. I suppose we owe it to the national good sense, that English Catholics have been protected from the extravagances which are elsewhere to be found. And we owe it also to the wisdom and moderation of the Holy See, which, in giving us the pattern for our devotion, as well as the rule of our faith, has never indulged in those curiosities of thought which are both so attractive to undisciplined imaginations and so dangerous to grovelling hearts. In the case of our own common people I think such a forced style of devotion would be simply unintelligible; as to the educated, I doubt whether it can have more than an occasional or temporary influence. If the Catholic faith spreads in England, these peculiarities will not spread with it. There is a healthy devotion to the Blessed Mary, and there is an artificial; it is possible to love her as a Mother, to honour her as a Virgin, to seek her as a Patron, and to exalt her as a Queen, without any injury to solid piety and Christian good sense:—I cannot help calling this the English style. I wonder whether you find any

thing to displease you in the Garden of the Soul, the Key of Heaven, the Vade Mecum, the Golden Manual, or the Crown of Jesus. These are the books to which Anglicans ought to appeal, who would be fair to us in this matter. I do not observe any thing in them which goes beyond the teaching of the Fathers, except so far as devotion goes beyond doctrine.

There is one collection of Devotions besides, of the highest authority, which has been introduced from abroad of late years. It consists of prayers of very various kinds which have been indulgenced by the Popes; and it commonly goes by the name of the *Raccolta*. As that word suggests, the language of many of the prayers is Italian, while others are in Latin. This circumstance is unfavourable to a translation, which, however skilful, must ever savour of the words and idioms of the original; but, passing over this necessary disadvantage, I consider there is hardly a clause in the good-sized volume in question which even the sensitiveness of English Catholicism would wish changed. Its anxious observance of doctrinal exactness is almost a fault. It seems afraid of using the words "give me," "make me," in its addresses to the Blessed Virgin, which are as natural to adopt, as in addressing a parent or friend. Surely we do not disparage Divine Providence when we say that we are indebted to our parents for our life, or when we ask their blessing; we do not show any atheistical leaning, because we say that a man's recovery must be left to nature, or that nature supplies brute animals with instincts. In like manner it seems to me a simple purism, to insist upon minute accuracy of expression in devotional and popular writings. However, the *Raccolta*, as coming from responsible authority, for the most part observes it. It commonly uses the phrases, "gain for us by thy prayers," "obtain for us," "pray to Jesus for me," "Speak for me, Mary," "carry thou our prayers," "ask for us grace," "intercede for the people of God," and the like, marking thereby with great emphasis that she is nothing more than an Advocate, and not a source of mercy. Nor do I recollect in this book more than one or two ideas to which you would be likely to raise an objection. The strongest of these is found in the Novena before her Nativity, in which, *apropos* of her Birth, we pray that she "would come down again, and be re-born spiritually in our souls;"—but it will occur to you that St. Paul speaks of his wish to impart to his converts, "not only the gospel, but his own soul;" and writing to the Corinthians, he says he has "begotten them by the gospel," and to Philemon, that he had "begotten Onesimus, in his bonds;" whereas St. James, with greater accuracy of expression, says "of His own will hath God begotten us with the word of truth." Again we find the petitioner saying to the Blessed Mary, "In thee I place all my hope;" but this is explained in another passage, "Thou art my best hope, after Jesus." Again, we read elsewhere, "I would I had a greater love for thee, since to love thee is a great mark of predestination;" but the prayer goes on, "Thy Son deserves of us an immeasurable love; pray that I may have this grace, a great love for Jesus," and further on, "I covet no good of the earth, but to love my God alone."

Then again, as to the lessons which our Catholics receive, whether by catechising or instruction, you would find nothing in our received manuals to which you would not assent, I am quite sure. Again, as to preaching, a standard book was drawn up three centuries ago, to supply matter for the purpose to the parochial clergy. You incidentally mention, p. 153, that the comment of Cornelius à Lapide on Scripture is "a repertorium for sermons;" but I never heard of this work being used, nor indeed can it, because of its size. The work provided for the purpose by the Church is the "Catechism of the Council of Trent," and nothing extreme about our Blessed Lady is propounded there. On the whole I am sanguine that you will come to the conclusion, that Anglicans may safely trust themselves to us English Catholics, as regards any devotions to the Blessed Virgin which might be required of them, over and above the rule of the Council of Trent.

6. And, now at length coming to the statements, not English, but foreign, which offend you in works written in her honour, I will frankly say that I read

some of those which you quote with grief and almost anger; for they seemed to me to ascribe to the Blessed Virgin a power of "searching the reins and hearts," which is the attribute of God alone; and I said to myself, how can we any more prove our Lord's divinity from Scripture, if those cardinal passages which invest Him with divine prerogatives, after all invest Him with nothing beyond what His Mother shares with Him? And how, again, is there any thing of incommunicable greatness in His death and passion, if He who was alone in the garden, alone upon the cross, alone in the resurrection, after all is not alone, but shared His solitary work with His Blessed Mother,—with her to whom, when He entered on His ministry, He said for our instruction, not as grudging her her proper glory, "Woman, what have I to do with thee?" And then again, if I hate those perverse sayings so much, how much more must she, in proportion to her love of Him? and how do we show our love for her, by wounding her in the very apple of her eye? This I said and say; but then on the other hand I have to observe that these strange words after all are but few in number, out of the many passages you cite; that most of them exemplify what I said above about the difficulty of determining the exact point where truth passes into error, and that they are allowable in one sense or connexion, and false in another. Thus to say that prayer (and the Blessed Virgin's prayer) is omnipotent, is a harsh expression in every-day prose; but, if it is explained to mean that there is nothing which prayer may not obtain from God, it is nothing else than the very promise made us in Scripture. Again, to say that Mary is the centre of all being, sounds inflated and profane; yet after all it is only one way, and a natural way, of saying that the Creator and the creature met together, and became one in her womb; and as such, I have used the expression above. Again, it is at first sight a paradox to say that "Jesus is obscured, because Mary is kept in the back-ground;" yet there is a sense, as I have shown above, in which it is a simple truth.

And so again certain statements may be true, under circumstances and in a particular time and place, which are abstractedly false; and hence it may be very unfair in a controversialist to interpret by an English or a modern rule, whatever may have been asserted by a foreign or mediæval author. To say, for instance, dogmatically, that no one can be saved without personal devotion to the Blessed Virgin, would be an untenable proposition; yet it might be true of this man or that, or of this or that country at this or that date; and if the very statement has ever been made by any writer of consideration (and this has to be ascertained), then perhaps it was made precisely under these exceptional circumstances. If an Italian preacher made it, I should feel no disposition to doubt him, at least as regards Italian youths and Italian maidens.

Then I think you have not always made your quotations with that consideration and kindness which is your rule. At p. 106, you say, "It is commonly said, that, if any Roman Catholic acknowledges that 'it is good and useful to pray to the saints,' he is not bound himself to do so. Were the above teaching true, it would be cruelty to say so; because, according to it, he would be forfeiting what is morally necessary to his salvation." But now, as to the fact, where is it said that to pray to our Lady and the Saints is necessary to salvation? The proposition of St. Alfonso is, that "God gives no grace except through Mary;" that is through her intercession. But intercession is one thing, devotion is another. And Suarez says, "It is the universal sentiment that the intercession of Mary is not only useful, but also in a certain manner necessary;" but still it is the question of her intercession, not of our invocation of her, not of devotion to her. If it were so, no Protestant could be saved; if it were so, there would be grave reasons for doubting of the salvation of St. Chrysostom or St. Athanasius, or of the primitive Martyrs; nay, I should like to know whether St. Augustine, in all his voluminous writings, invokes her once. Our Lord died for those heathens who did not know Him; and His Mother intercedes for those Christians who do not know her; and she intercedes according to His will, and, when He wills to save a particular soul, she at once prays for it. I say, He wills indeed according to her prayer, but then she prays according to His will. Though then it is natural and prudent for those to have recourse to her, who from the Church's teaching know her power, yet it cannot be said that devotion to her is a *sine-quâ-non* of salvation. Some indeed of the authors, whom you quote, go further; they do speak of devotion; but even then, they do not enunciate the general proposition which I have been disallowing. For instance, they say, "It is morally impossible for those to be saved who *neglect* the devotion to the Blessed Virgin;" but a simple omission is one thing, and neglect another. "It is impossible for any to be saved who *turns away* from her," yes; but to "turn away" is to offer some positive disrespect or insult towards her, and that with sufficient knowledge; and I certainly think it would be a very grave act, if in a Catholic country (and of such the writers were speaking, for they knew of no other), with Ave-Marias sounding in the air, and images of the Madonna in every street and road, a Catholic broke off or gave up a practice that was universal, and in which he was brought up, and deliberately put her name out of his thoughts.

7. Though, then, common sense may determine for us, that the line of prudence and propriety has been certainly passed in the instance of certain statements about the Blessed Virgin, it is often not easy to prove the point logically; and in such cases

authority, if it attempt to act, would be in the position which so often happens in our courts of law, when the commission of an offence is morally certain, but the government prosecutor cannot find legal evidence sufficient to ensure conviction. I am not denying the right of Sacred Congregations, at their will, to act peremptorily, and without assigning reasons for the judgment they pass upon writers; but, when they have found it inexpedient to take this severe course, perhaps it may happen from the circumstances of the case, that there is no other that they can take, even if they would. It is wiser then for the most part to leave these excesses to the gradual operation of public opinion, that is, to the opinion of educated and sober Catholics; and this seems to me the healthiest way of putting them down. Yet in matter of fact I believe the Holy See has interfered from time to time, when devotion seemed running into superstition; and not so long ago. I recollect hearing in Gregory the XVI.'s time, of books about the Blessed Virgin, which had been suppressed by authority; and in particular of a representation of the Immaculate Conception which he had forbidden, and of measures taken against the shocking notion that the Blessed Mary is present in the Holy Eucharist, in the sense in which our Lord is present; but I have no means of verifying the information I received.

Nor have I time, any more than you have had, to ascertain how far great theologians have made protests against those various extravagances of which you so rightly complain. Passages, however, from three well-known Jesuit Fathers have opportunely come in my way, and in one of them is introduced in confirmation, the name of the great Gerson. They are Canisius, Petavius, and Raynaudus; and as they speak very appositely, and you do not seem to know them, I will here make some extracts from them:—

(1.) Canisius:—

"We confess that in the *cultus* of Mary it has been, and is possible for corruptions to creep in; and we have a more than ordinary desire that the Pastors of the Church should be carefully vigilant here, and give no place to Satan, whose characteristic office it has ever been, while men sleep, to sow the cockle amid the Lord's wheat.... For this purpose it is his wont gladly to avail himself of the aid of heretics, fanatics, and false Catholics, as may be seen in the instance of this *Marianus cultus*. This *cultus*, heretics, suborned by Satan, attack with hostility. . . . Thus too, certain mad heads are so demented by Satan, as to embrace superstitions and idolatries instead of the true *cultus*, and neglect altogether the due measures whether in respect to God or to Mary. Such indeed were the Collyridians of old. . . . Such that German herdsman a hundred years ago, who gave out publicly that he was a new prophet, and had had a vision of the Deipara, and told the people in her name to pay no more tributes and taxes to princes. . . . Moreover, how many Catholics does one see who, by great and shocking negligence, have neither care nor regard for her *cultus*, but, given to profane and secular objects, scarce once a year raise their earthly minds to sing her praises or to venerate her?"—*De Mariâ Deiparâ*, p. 518.

(2.) Father Petau says, when discussing the teaching of the Fathers about the Blessed Virgin (*de Incarn.* xiv. 8.)—

"I will venture to give this advice to all who would be devout and panegyrical towards the Holy Virgin, viz. not to exceed in their piety and devotion to her, but to be content with true and solid praises, and to cast aside what is otherwise. The latter kind of idolatry, lurking, as St. Augustine says, nay implanted in human hearts, is greatly abhorrent from Theology, that is, from the gravity of heavenly wisdom, which never thinks or asserts any thing, but what is measured by certain and accurate rules. What that rule should be, and what caution is to be used in our present subject, I will not determine of myself; but according to the mind of a most weighty and most learned theologian, John Gerson, who in one of his Epistles proposes certain canons, which he calls truths, by means of which are to be measured the assertions of theologians concerning the Incarnation . . . . . . By these truly golden precepts Gerson brings within bounds the immoderate licence of praising the Blessed Virgin, and restrains it within the measure of sober and healthy piety. And from these it is evident that that sort of reasoning is frivolous and nugatory, in which so many indulge, in order to assign any sort of grace they please, however unusual, to the Blessed Virgin. For they argue thus; 'Whatever the Son of God could bestow for the glory of His Mother, that it became Him in fact to furnish;' or again, 'Whatever honours or ornaments He has poured out on other saints, those all together hath He heaped upon His Mother;' whence they draw their chain of reasoning to their desired conclusion; a mode of argumentation which Gerson treats with contempt as captious and sophistical."

He adds, what of course we all should say, that, in thus speaking, he has no intention to curtail the liberty of pious persons in such meditations and conjectures, on the mysteries of faith, sacred histories and the Scripture text, as are of the nature of comments, supplements, and the like.

(3.) Raynaud is an author, full of devotion, if any one is so, to the Blessed Virgin; yet in the work which he has composed in her honour (*Diptycha Mariana*), he says more than I can quote here, to the same purpose as Petau. I abridge some portions of his text:—

"Let this be taken for granted, that no praises of ours can come up to the praises due to the Virgin Mother. But we must not make up for our inability to reach her true praise, by a supply of lying embellishment and false honours. For there are some whose affection for religious objects is so imprudent and lawless, that they transgress the due limits even towards the saints. This Origen has excellently observed upon in the case of the Baptist, for very many, instead of observing the measure of charity, considered whether he might not be the Christ." p. 9. "... St. Anselm, the first, or one of the first champions of the public celebration of the Blessed Virgin's Immaculate Conception, says, *de Excell. Virg.*, that the Church considers it indecent, that any thing that admits of doubt should be said in her praise, when the things which are certainly true of her supply such large materials for laudation. It is right so to interpret St. Epiphanius also, when he says that human tongues should not pronounce any thing lightly of the Deipara; and who is more justly to be charged with speaking lightly of the most holy Mother of God, than he, who, as if what is certain and evident did not suffice for her full investiture, is wiser than the aged, and obtrudes on us the toadstools of his own mind, and devotions unheard of by those Holy Fathers who loved her best? Plainly, as St. Anselm says, that she is the Mother of God, this by itself exceeds every elevation which can be named or imagined, short of God. About so sublime a majesty we should not speak hastily from prurience of wit, or flimsy pretext of promoting piety; but with great maturity of thought; and, whenever the maxims of the Church and the oracles of faith do not suffice, then not without the suffrages of the Doctors . . . . . Those who are subject to this prurience of innovation, do not perceive how broad is the difference between subjects of human science, and heavenly things. All novelty concerning the objects of our faith is to be put far away;

except so far as by diligent investigation of God's Word, written and unwritten, and a well founded inference from what is thence to be elicited, something is brought to light which though already indeed there, had not hitherto been recognized. The innovations which we condemn are those which rest neither on the written nor unwritten Word, nor on conclusions from it, nor on the judgment of ancient sages, nor sufficient basis of reason, but on the sole colour and pretext of doing more honour to the Deipara."—p. 10.

In another portion of the same work, he speaks in particular of one of those imaginations to which you especially refer, and for which, without strict necessity (as it seems to me) you allege the authority of à Lapide.

" Nor is that honour of the Deipara to be offered, viz. that the elements of the body of Christ, which the Blessed Virgin supplied to it, remain perpetually unaltered in Christ, and thereby are found also in the Eucharist . . . . . This solicitude for the Virgin's glory, must, I consider, be discarded; since, if rightly considered, it involves an injury towards Christ, and such honours the Virgin loveth not. And first, dismissing philosophical bagatelles about the animation of blood, milk, &c., who can endure the proposition that a good portion of the substance of Christ in the Eucharist should be worshipped with a *cultus* less than *latria?* viz. by the inferior *cultus* of *hyperdulia?* The preferable class of theologians contend that not even the humanity of Christ, is to be materially abstracted from the Word of God, and worshipped by itself; how then shall we introduce a *cultus* of the Deipara in Christ, which is inferior to the *cultus* proper to Him ? How is this other than a casting down of the substance of Christ from His Royal Throne, and a degradation of it to some inferior sitting place ? It is nothing to the purpose to refer to such Fathers, as say that the flesh of Christ is the flesh of Mary, for they speak of its origin. What will hinder, if this doctrine be admitted, our also admitting that there is something in Christ which is detestable? for, as the first elements of a body which were communicated by the Virgin to Christ, have (as these authors say) remained perpetually in Christ, so the same *materia*, at least in part, which belonged originally to the ancestors of Christ, came down to the Virgin from her father, unchanged, and taken from her grandfather, and so on. And thus, since it is not unlikely that some of these ancestors were reprobate, there would now be something actually in Christ, which had belonged to a reprobate, and worthy of detestation."—p. 237.

8. After such explanations, and with such authorities, to clear my path, I put away from me, as you would wish, without any hesitation, as matters in which my heart and reason have no part, (when taken in their literal and absolute sense, as any Protestant would naturally take them, and as the writers doubtless did not use them,) such sentences, and phrases, as these:—that the mercy of Mary is infinite; that God has resigned into her hands His omnipotence; that (unconditionally) it is safer to seek her than her Son; that the Blessed Virgin is superior to God; that He is (simply) subject to her command; that our Lord is now of the same disposition as His Father towards sinners, viz. a disposition to reject them, while Mary takes His place as an Advocate with Father and Son; that the Saints are more ready to intercede with Jesus than Jesus with the Father; that Mary is the only refuge of those with whom God is angry; that Mary alone can obtain a Protestant's conversion; that it would have sufficed for the salvation of men if our Lord had died, not

to obey His Father, but to defer to the decree of His mother; that she rivals our Lord in being God's daughter, not by adoption, but by a kind of nature; that Christ fulfilled the office of Saviour by imitating her virtues; that, as the Incarnate God bore the image of His Father, so He bore the image of His Mother; that redemption derived from Christ indeed its sufficiency, but from Mary its beauty and loveliness; that as we are clothed with the merits of Christ so we are clothed with the merits of Mary; that, as He is Priest in a like sense is she Priestess; that His Body and Blood in the Eucharist are truly hers and appertain to her; that as He is present and received therein, so is she present and received therein; that Priests are ministers as of Christ, so of Mary; that elect souls are born of God and Mary; that the Holy Ghost brings into fruitfulness his action by her, producing in her and by her Jesus Christ in His members; that the kingdom of God in our souls, as our Lord speaks, is really the kingdom of Mary in the soul—and she and the Holy Ghost produce in the soul extraordinary things—and when the Holy Ghost finds Mary in a soul He flies there.

Sentiments such as these I never knew of till I read your book, nor, as I think, do the vast majority of English Catholics know them. They seem to me like a bad dream. I could not have conceived them to be said. I know not to what authority to go for them, to Scripture, or to the Fathers, or to the decrees of Councils, or to the consent of schools, or to the tradition of the faithful, or to the Holy See, or to Reason. They defy all the *loci theologici*. There is nothing of them in the Missal, in the Roman Catechism, in the Roman *Raccolta*, in the Imitation of Christ, in Gother, Challoner, Milner, or Wiseman, as far as I am aware. They do but scare and confuse me. I should not be holier, more spiritual, more sure of perseverance, if I twisted my moral being into the reception of them; I should but be guilty of fulsome frigid flattery towards the most upright and noble of God's creatures, if I professed them,—and of stupid flattery too; for it would be like the compliment of painting up a young and beautiful princess with the brow of a Plato and the muscle of an Achilles. And I should expect her to tell one of her people in waiting to turn me off her service without warning. Whether thus to feel be the *scandalum parvulorum* in my case, or the *scandalum Pharisæorum*, I leave others to decide; but I will say plainly that I had rather believe (which is impossible) that there is no God at all, than that Mary is greater than God. I will have nothing to do with statements, which can only be explained, by being explained away. I do not, however, speak of these statements, as they are found in their authors, for I know nothing of the originals, and cannot believe that they have meant what you say; but I take them as they lie in your pages. Were any of them the sayings of Saints in ecstasy, I should know they had a good meaning; still I should not repeat them myself; but I am looking at them, not as spoken by the tongues of Angels, but according to that literal sense which they bear in the mouths of English men and English women. And, as spoken by man to man, in England, in the nineteenth century, I consider them calculated to prejudice inquirers, to frighten the unlearned, to unsettle consciences, to provoke blasphemy, and to work the loss of souls.

9. And now, after having said so much as this, bear with me, my dear Friend, if I end with an expostulation. Have you not been touching us on a very tender point in a very rude way? is not the effect of what you have said to expose her to scorn and obloquy? who is dearer to us than any other creature? Have you even hinted that our love for her is any thing else than an abuse? Have you thrown her one kind word yourself all through your book? I trust so, but I have not lighted upon one. And yet I know you love her well. Can you wonder, then,—can I complain, much, much as I grieve,—that men should utterly misconceive of you, and are blind to the fact that you have put the whole argument between you and us on a new footing; and that, whereas it was said twenty-five years ago in the British Critic, "Till Rome ceases to be what practically she is, union is *impossible* between her and England," you declare on the contrary,

"Union *is possible*, as soon as Italy and England, having the same faith and the same centre of unity, are allowed to hold severally their own theological opinions?" They have not done you justice here; because in truth, the honour of our Lady is dearer to them than the conversion of England.

Take a parallel case, and consider how you would decide it yourself. Supposing an opponent of a doctrine for which you so earnestly contend, the eternity of punishment, instead of meeting you with direct arguments against it, heaped together a number of extravagant descriptions of the place, mode and circumstances of its infliction, quoted Tertullian as a witness for the primitive Fathers, and the Covenanters and Ranters for these last centuries; brought passages from the Inferno of Dante, and from the Sermons of Wesley and Whitfield; nay, supposing he confined himself to the chapters on the subject in the work, which has the sanction of Jeremy Taylor, on " The State of Man," or to his Sermon on the Foolish Exchange, or to passages in Leighton, South, Beveridge, and Barrow, would you think this a fair and becoming method of reasoning? and, if he avowed that he should ever consider the Anglican Church committed to all these accessories of the doctrine, till its authorities formally denounced Taylor, and Whitfield, and a hundred others, would you think this an equitable determination, or the procedure of a theologian?

So far concerning the Blessed Virgin; the chief but not the only subject of your Volume. And now, when I could wish to proceed, she seems to stop me, for the Feast of her Immaculate Conception is upon us; and close upon its Octave, which is kept with special solemnities in the Churches of this town, come the great Antiphons, the heralds of Christmas. That joyful season, joyful for all of us, while it centres in Him who then came on earth, also brings before us in peculiar prominence that Virgin Mother, who bore and nursed Him. Here she is not in the background, as at Easter-tide, but she brings Him to us in her arms. Two great Festivals, dedicated to her honour, to-morrow's and the Purification, mark out and keep the ground, and, like the towers of David, open the way to and fro, for the high holiday season of the Prince of Peace. And all along it her image is upon it, such as we see it in the typical representation of the Catacombs. May the sacred influences of this time bring us all together in unity! May it destroy all bitterness on your side and ours! May it quench all jealous, sour, proud, fierce antagonism on our side; and dissipate all captious, carping, fastidious refinements of reasoning on yours! May that bright and gentle Lady, the Blessed Virgin Mary, overcome you with her sweetness, and revenge herself on her foes by interceding effectually for their conversion!

I am,

Yours, most affectionately,

JOHN H. NEWMAN.

The Oratory, Birmingham,
*In fest. S. Ambrosii,* 1865.

# NOTES.

### NOTE. A.   PAGE 36.

1. St. Justin:—Υἱὸν Θεοῦ γεγραμμένον αὐτὸν ἐν τοῖς ἀπομνημονεύμασι τῶν ἀποστόλων αὐτοῦ ἔχοντες, καὶ υἱὸν αὐτὸν λέγοντες, νενοήκαμεν, καὶ πρὸ πάντων ποιημάτων ἀπὸ τοῦ πατρὸς δυνάμει αὐτοῦ καὶ βουλῇ προελθόντα .... καὶ διὰ τῆς παρθένου ἄνθρωπος[ον] γεγονέναι, ἵνα καὶ δι᾽ ἧς ὁδοῦ ἡ ἀπὸ τοῦ ὄφεως παρακοὴ τὴν ἀρχὴν ἔλαβε, καὶ διὰ ταύτης τῆς ὁδοῦ καὶ κατάλυσιν λάβῃ· παρθένος γὰρ οὖσα Εὔα καὶ ἄφθορος τὸν λόγον τὸν ἀπὸ τοῦ ὄφεως συλλαβοῦσα, παρακοὴν καὶ θάνατον ἔτεκε· πίστιν δὲ καὶ χαρὰν λαβοῦσα Μαρία ἡ παρθένος, εὐαγγελιζομένου αὐτῇ Γαβριὴλ ἀγγέλου, ὅτι Πνεῦμα Κυρίου ἐπ᾽ αὐτὴν ἐπελεύσεται, &c. .... ἀπεκρίνατο, Γένοιτό μοι κατὰ τὸ ῥῆμά σου.—*Tryph.* 100.

2. Tertullian:—" Ne mihi vacet incursus nominis Adæ, unde Christus Adam ab Apostolo dictus est, si terreni non fuit census homo ejus? Sed et hic ratio defendit, quod Deus imaginem et similitudinem suam a diabolo captam æmula operatione recuperavit.  In virginem enim adhuc Evam irrepserat verbum ædificatorium mortis. In virginem æque introducendum erat Dei verbum extructorium vitæ; ut quod per ejusmodi sexum abierat in perditionem, per eundem sexum redigeretur in salutem.  Crediderat Eva serpenti; credidit Maria Gabrieli; quod illa credendo deliquit, hæc credendo delevit."—*De Carn. Chr.* 17.

3. St. Irenæus:—" Consequenter autem et Maria virgo obediens invenitur, dicens, ecce ancilla tua, Domine, fiat mihi secundum verbum tuum.  Eva vero inobediens: non obedivit

enim, adhuc quum esset virgo. Quemadmodum illa, virum quidem habens Adam, virgo tamen adhuc existens (erant enim utrique nudi in Paradiso, et non confundebantur, quoniam, paullo ante facti, non intellectum habebant filiorum generationis; oportebat enim illos primo adolescere, dehinc sic multiplicari), inobediens facta, et sibi et universo generi humano causa facta est mortis: sic et Maria, habens prædestinatum virum, et tamen virgo, obediens, et sibi et universo generi humano causa facta est salutis. Et propter hoc Lex eam, quæ desponsata erat viro, licet virgo sit adhuc, uxorem ejus, qui desponsaverat, vocat; eam quæ est à Maria in Evam recirculationem significans: quia non aliter quod colligatum est solveretur, nisi ipsæ compagines alligationis reflectantur retrorsus; ut primæ conjunctiones solvantur per secundas, secundæ rursus liberent primas. Et evenit primam quidem compaginem à secundâ colligatione solvere, secundam vero colligationem primæ solutionis habere locum. Et propter hoc Dominus dicebat, primos quidem novissimos futuros, et novissimos primos. Et propheta autem hoc idem significat, dicens, 'Pro patribus nati sunt tibi filii.' 'Primogenitus' enim 'mortuorum' natus Dominus, et in sinum suum recipiens pristinos patres, regeneravit eos in vitam Dei, ipse initium viventium factus, quoniam Adam initium morientium factus est. Propter hoc et Lucas initium generationis a Domino inchoans, in Adam retulit, significans, quoniam non illi hunc, sed hic illos in Evangelium vitæ regeneravit. Sic autem et Evæ inobedientiæ nodus solutionem accepit per obedientiam Mariæ. Quod enim alligavit virgo Eva per incredulitatem, hoc virgo Maria solvit per fidem."—*S. Iren. contr. Hær.* iii. 22.

"Quemadmodum enim illa per Angeli sermonem seducta est, ut effugeret Deum, prævaricata verbum ejus; ita et hæc per Angelicum sermonem evangelizata est, ut portaret Deum, obediens ejus verbo. Et si ea inobedierat Deo; sed hæc suasa est obedire Deo, uti Virginis Evæ Virgo Maria fieret advocata. Et quemadmodum adstrictum est morti genus humanum per Virginem, salvatur per Virginem, æqua lance disposita, virginalis inobedientia, per virginalem obedientiam."—*Ibid.* v. 19.

4. St. Cyril:—Διὰ παρθένου τῆς Εὔας ἦλθεν ὁ θάνατος, ἔδει διὰ παρθένου, μᾶλλον δὲ ἐκ παρθένου, φανῆναι τὴν ζωήν· ἵνα ὥσπερ

ἐκείνην ὄφις ἠπάτησεν, οὕτω καὶ ταύτην Γαβριὴλ εὐαγγελίσηται.—
*Cat.* xii. 15.

5. St. Ephrem.:—"Per Evam nempe decora et amabilis hominis gloria extincta est, quæ tamen rursus per Mariam refloruit."—*Opp. Syr.* ii. p. 318.

"Initio protoparentum delicto in omnes homines mors pertransiit; hodie vero per Mariam translati sumus de morte ad vitam. Initio serpens, Evæ auribus occupatis, inde virus in totum corpus dilatavit; hodie Maria ex auribus perpetuæ felicitatis assertorem excepit. Quod ergo mortis fuit, simul et vitæ extitit instrumentum."—iii. p. 607.

6. St. EPIPHANIUS:—Αὐτὴ ἐστὶν ἡ παρὰ μὲν τῇ Εὔᾳ σημαινομένη δι' αἰνίγματος λαβοῦσα τὸ καλεῖσθαι μήτηρ ζώντων. . . . καὶ ἦν θαῦμα ὅτι μετὰ τὴν παράβασιν ταύτην τὴν μεγάλην ἔσχεν ἐπωνυμίαν. καὶ κατὰ μὲν τὸ αἰσθητὸν, ἀπ' ἐκείνης τῆς Εὔας πᾶσα τῶν ἀνθρώπων ἡ γέννησις ἐπὶ γῆς γεγέννηται· ὧδε δὲ ἀληθῶς ἀπὸ Μαρίας αὐτὴ ἡ ζωὴ τῷ κόσμῳ γεγέννηται· ἵνα ζῶντα γεννήσῃ, καὶ γέννηται ἡ Μαρία μήτηρ ζώντων· δι' αἰνίγματος οὖν ἡ Μαρία μήτηρ ζώντων κέκληται . . . ἀλλὰ καὶ ἕτερον περὶ τούτων διανοεῖσθαί ἐστι θαυμαστὸν, περὶ δὲ τῆς Εὔας καὶ τῆς Μαρίας· ἡ μὲν γὰρ Εὔα πρόφασις γεγέννηται θανάτου τοῖς ἀνθρώποις· . . . ἡ δὲ Μαρία πρόφασις ζωῆς . . . ἵνα ζωὴ ἀντὶ θανάτου γέννηται, ἐκκλείσασα τὸν θάνατον τὸν ἐκ γυναικὸς, πάλιν ὁ διὰ γυναικὸς ἡμῖν ζωὴ γεγεννημένος.—*Hær.* 78. 18.

7. St. Jerome:—"Postquam vero Virgo concepit in utero, et peperit nobis puerum . . . soluta maledictio est. Mors per Evam, vita per Mariam."—*Ep.* 22, *ad Eustochium*, 21.

8. St. Augustine:—"Huc accedit magnum sacramentum, ut, quoniam per feminam nobis mors acciderat, vita nobis per feminam nasceretur: ut de utrâque naturâ, id est, femininâ et masculinâ, victus diabolus cruciaretur, quoniam de ambarum subversione lætabatur, cui parum fuerat ad pœnam si ambæ naturæ in nobis liberarentur, nisi etiam per ambas liberaremur."
—*De Agone Christ.* 24.

9. St. Peter Chrysologus:—"Benedicta tu in mulieribus. Quia in quibus Eva maledicta puniebat viscera; tunc in illis gaudet, honoratur, suspicitur Maria benedicta. Et facta est vere nunc mater viventium per gratiam quæ mater extitit morientium per naturam. . . . Quantus sit Deus satis ignorat ille, qui hujus Virginis mentem non stupet, animum non miratur:

pavet cœlum, tremunt Angeli, creatura non sustinet, natura non sufficit, et una puella sic Deum in sui pectoris capit, recipit, oblectat hospitio, ut pacem terris, cœlis gloriam, salutem perditis, vitam mortuis, terrenis cum cœlestibus parentelam, ipsius Dei cum carne commercium, pro ipsa domus exigat pensione, pro ipsius uteri mercede conquirat, et impleat illud Prophetæ: Ecce hæreditas Domini, filii merces fructus ventris. Sed jam se concludat sermo ut de partu Virginis, donante Deo, et indulgente tempore, gratius proloquamur."—*Serm.* 140.

10. St. Fulgentius:—"In primi hominis conjuge, nequitia diaboli seductam depravavit mentem : in secundi autem hominis matre, gratia Dei, et mentem integram servavit, et carnem : menti contulit firmissimam fidem, carni abstulit omnino libidinem. Quoniam igitur miserabiliter pro peccato damnatus est homo, ideo sine peccato mirabiliter natus est Deus homo."—*Serm.* ii.

"Venite, virgines, ad virginem; venite, concipientes, ad concipientem; venite, parturientes, ad parturientem; venite, matres, ad matrem; venite, lactantes, ad lactantem; venite, juvenculæ, ad juvenculam. Ideo omnes istos cursus naturæ virgo Maria in Domino nostro Jesu Christo suscepit, ut omnibus ad se confugientibus fœminis subveniret, et sic restauraret omne genus fœminarum ad se advenientium nova Eva servando virginitatem, sicut omne genus virorum Adam novus recuperat dominus Jesus Christus."—*Ibid.* iii.

P.S. Third Edition: A friend reminds me that I have omitted, among the instances of the comparison of Eve with Mary, the passage at the end of the Epistle to Diognetus, a testimony most important from the great antiquity of that work, from the religious beauty of its composition, and the stress laid upon it by Protestants.

I should also observe, that, at the end of the last extract from St. Irenæus, p. 126, "solvatur" is found in some MSS. for "salvatur." Vid. Ed. Bened. And so St. Augustine contr. Jul. i. n. 5. Ed. Bened. This various reading does not affect the general sense of the passage.

## NOTE B.  PAGE 49.

Abridged from Suarez.  Opp. t. 17, p. 7—Ed. Venet. 1746 :—

"1. Statuendum est B. Virginem fuisse a Christo redemptam, quia Christus fuit universalis redemptor totius generis humani, et pro omnibus hominibus mortuus est."—p. 15.

"2. Præterea constat indiguisse Virginem redemptione, quia nimirum descendebat ex Adamo per seminalem generationem."—p. 7.

"3. Tanquam certum statuendum est, B. Virginem procreatam esse ex viri et fœminæ commixtione carnali, ad modum aliorum hominum.  Habetur certâ traditione et communi consensu totius Ecclesiæ."—p. 7.

"4. Absolute et simpliciter fatendum B. Virginem in Adam peccasse."—p. 16.

"5. B. Virgo peccavit in Adamo, ex quo tanquam ex radice infecta per seminalem rationem est orta; hæc est tota ratio contrahendi originale peccatum, quod est ex vi conceptionis, nisi gratiâ Dei præveniat."—p. 16.

"6. Certum est B. Virginem fuisse mortuam saltem in Adamo.  Sicut in Christo vitam habuit, ita et in Adam fuit mortua.  Alias B. Virgo non contraxisset mortem aliasve corporis pœnalitates ex Adamo; consequens [autem] est omnino falsum.  Habuit B. Virgo meritum mortis saltem in Adamo.  Illa vere habuit mortem carnis ex peccato Adami contractam."—p. 16.

"7. B. Virgo, ex vi suæ conceptionis fuit obnoxia originali peccato, seu debitum habuit contrahendi illud, nisi divinâ gratiâ fuisset impeditum."—p. 16.

"8. Si B. Virgo non fuisset (ut ita dicam) vendita in Adamo, et de se servituti peccati obnoxia, non fuisset vere redempta."—p. 16.

"9. Dicendum est, potuisse B. Virginem præservari ab originali peccato, et in primo suæ conceptionis instanti sanctificari."—p. 17.

"10. Potuit B. Virgo ex vi suæ originis esse obnoxia culpæ, et ideo indigere redemptione, et nihilominus in eodem momento, in quo erat obnoxia, præveniri, ne illam contraheret."—p. 14.

"11. Dicendum B. Virginem in ipso primo instanti conceptionis suæ fuisse sanctificatam, et ab originali peccato præservatam."—p. 19.

"12. Carnem Virginis fuisse carnem peccati ... verum est, non quia illa caro aliquando fuit subdita peccato, aut informata anima carente gratia, sed quia fuit mortalis et passibilis ex debito peccati, cui de se erat obnoxia, si per Christi gratiam non fuisset præservata."—p. 22.

"13. Quod B. Virgo de se fuerit obnoxia peccato, (si illud revera nunquam habuit,) non derogat perfectæ ejus sanctitati et puritati."—pp. 16, 17.

Cornelius à Lapide, Comment. in Ep. ad Rom. v. 12 :—

"The Blessed Virgin sinned in Adam, and incurred this necessity of contracting original sin; but original sin itself she did not contract in herself in fact, nor had it; for she was anticipated by the grace of God, which excluded all sin from her, in the first moment of her conception."

In 2 Ep. ad Corinth. v. 15 :—

"All died, namely in Adam, for in him all contracted the necessity of sin and death, even the Deipara; so that both herself and man altogether needed Christ as a Redeemer and His death. Therefore the Blessed Virgin sinned and died in Adam, but in her own person she contracted not sin and the death of the soul, for she was anticipated by God and God's grace."

Third Edition: If any one wishes to see our doctrine drawn out in a Treatise of the present day, he should have recourse to Dr. Ullathorne's Exposition of the Immaculate Conception, a work full of instruction and of the first authority.

## NOTE C.  PAGE 53.

I have allowed that several great Fathers of the Church, of the fourth and fifth centuries, speak of the Blessed Virgin in terms, which we never should think of using now, and which at first sight are inconsistent with the belief and sentiment concerning her, which I have ascribed to their times. These Fathers are St. Basil, St. Chrysostom, and St. Cyril of Alexandria; and the occasion of their so speaking is furnished by certain passages of Scripture, on which they are commenting. It may in consequence be asked of me, why I do not take these three, instead of St. Justin, St. Irenæus, and Tertullian, as my authoritative basis for determining the doctrine of the primitive times concerning the Blessed Mary: why, instead of making St. Irenæus, &c. the rule, and St. Basil, &c. the exception, I do not make the earlier Fathers the exception, and the later the rule. Since I do not, it may be urged against me that I am but making a case for my own opinion, and playing the part of an advocate.

Now I do not see that it would be illogical or nugatory, though I did nothing more than make a case; indeed I have worded myself in my Letter as if I wished to do little more. For as much as this is surely to the purpose, considering the majority of Anglicans have a supreme confidence that no case whatever can be made in behalf of our doctrine concerning the Blessed Virgin from the ancient Fathers. I should have gained a real point, if I did any thing to destroy this imagination; but I intend to attempt something more than this. I shall attempt to invalidate the only grounds on which any teaching contrary to the Catholic can be founded on Antiquity.

I. First I set down the passages which create the difficulty, as they are found in the great work of Petavius, a theologian too candid and fearless, to put out of sight or explain away adverse facts, from fear of scandal, or from the expedience of controversy.

1. St. Basil then writes thus, in his 260th Epistle, addressed to Optimus:—

"[Symeon] uses the word 'sword,' meaning the word which is tentative and critical of the thoughts, and reaches unto the separation of soul and spirit, of the joints and marrow. Since then every soul, at the time of the Passion, was subjected in a way to some unsettlement (διακρίσει), according to the Lord's word, who said, 'All ye shall be scandalized in Me,' Symeon prophesies even of Mary herself, that, standing by the Cross, and seeing what was doing, and hearing the words, after the testimony of Gabriel, after the secret knowledge of the divine conception, after the great manifestation of miracles, Thou wilt experience, he says, a certain tossing (σάλος) of thy soul. For it beseemed the Lord to taste death for every one, and to become a propitiation of the world, in order to justify all in His blood. And thee thyself who hast been taught from above the things concerning the Lord, some unsettlement (διάκρισις) will reach. This is the sword; 'that out of many hearts thoughts may be revealed.' He obscurely signifies, that, after the scandalizing which took place upon the Cross of Christ, both to the disciples and to Mary herself, some quick healing should follow upon it from the Lord, confirming their heart unto faith in Him."

2. St. Chrysostom, in Matth. Hom. iv.:—

"'Wherefore,' a man may say, 'did not the angel do in the case of the Virgin, [what he did to Joseph?'" viz. appear to her after, not before, the Incarnation,] "'why did he not bring her the good tidings after her conception?' lest she should be in great disturbance and trouble. For the probability was, that, had she not known the clear fact, she would have resolved something strange (ἄτοπον) about herself, and had recourse to rope or sword, not bearing the disgrace. For the Virgin was admirable, and Luke shows her virtue, when he says that, when she heard the salutation, she did not at once become extravagant, nor appropriated the words, but was troubled, searching what was the nature of the salutation. One then of so accurately formed a mind (διηκριβωμένη) would be made beside herself with despondency, considering the disgrace, and not expecting, whatever she may say, to persuade any one who hears her, that adultery had not been the fact. Lest then these things occur, the Angel came before the conception; for it beseemed that that womb should be without disorder, which the Creator of all entered, and that that soul should be rid of all perturbation, which was counted worthy to become the minister of such mysteries."

In Matth. Hom. xliv. (vid. also in Joann. Hom. xxi.):—

"To-day we learn something else even further, viz., that not even to bear Christ in the womb, and to have that wonderful childbirth, has any gain, without virtue. And this is especially true from this passage, 'As He was yet speaking to the multitude, behold His Mother and His brethren stood without, seeking to speak to Him,' &c. This he said, not as ashamed of His Mother, nor as denying her who bore Him; for, had He been ashamed, He had not passed through that womb; but as showing that there was no profit to her thence, unless she did all that was necessary. For what she attempted, came of overmuch love of honour; for she wished to show to the people that she had power and authority over her Son, in nothing ever as yet having been greatly ostentatious (φανταζομένη) about Him. Therefore she came thus unseasonably. Observe then her and their recklessness (ἀπόνοιαν). . . . Had He wished to deny His Mother, then He would have denied, when the Jews taunted Him with her. But no; He shows such care of her as to commit her as a legacy on the Cross itself to the disciple whom He loved best of all, and to take anxious oversight of her. But does He not do the same now, by caring for her and His brethren? . . . And consider, not only the words which convey the considerate rebuke, but also . . . who He is who utters it, . . . and what He aims at in uttering it, not, that is, as wishing to cast her into perplexity, but to release her from a most tyrannical affection, and to bring her gradually to the fitting thought concerning Him, and to persuade her that He is not only her Son, but also her Master."

3. St. Cyril, in Joann. lib. xii.:—

"How shall we explain this passage? He introduces both His Mother and the other women with her standing at the Cross, and, as is plain, weeping. For somehow the race of women is ever fond of tears; and especially given to laments, when it has rich occasions for weeping. How then did they persuade the blessed Evangelist to be so minute in his account, so as to make mention of this abidance of the women? For it was his purpose to teach even this, viz., that probably even the Mother of the Lord herself was scandalized at the unexpected Passion, and that the death upon the Cross, being so very bitter, was near unsettling her from her fitting mind; and in addition to this, the mockeries of the Jews, and the soldiers too, perhaps, who were sitting near the Cross and making a jest of Him who was hanging on it, and daring, in the sight of His very mother, the division of His garments. Doubt not that she received (εἰσεδέξατο) some such thoughts as these:—I bore Him who is laughed at on the wood; but, in saying He was the true Son of the Omnipotent God, perhaps somehow He was mistaken. He said He was the Life, how then has He been crucified? how has He been strangled by the cords of His murderers? how prevailed He not over the plot of His persecutors? why descends He not from the Cross, though He bade Lazarus to return to life, and amazed all Judæa with His miracles? And it is very natural that a woman (τὸ γύναιον, woman's nature), not knowing the mystery, should slide into some such trains of thought. For we should understand, if we do well, that the gravity of the circumstances was enough to overturn even a self-possessed mind; it is no wonder then if a woman (τὸ γύναιον) slipped into this reasoning. For if he himself, the chosen one of the holy disciples, Peter, once was scandalized, . . . so as to cry out hastily, Be it far from Thee, Lord. . . . what paradox is it, if the soft mind of womankind was carried off to weak ideas? And this we say, not idly conjecturing, as it may strike one, but entertaining the suspicion from what is written concerning the Mother of the Lord. For we remember that Simeon the Just, when he received the Lord as a little child into his arms, . . . said to her, 'A sword shall go through thine own soul, that out of many hearts thoughts may be revealed.' By sword he meant the sharp access of suffering cutting down a woman's mind into extravagant thoughts. For temptations test the hearts of those who suffer them, and make bare the thoughts which are in them."

Now what do these three Fathers say in these passages?
1. St. Basil imputes to the Blessed Virgin, not only doubt, but the sin of doubt. On the other hand, 1. he imputes it only on one occasion; 2. he does not consider it to be a grave sin; 3. he implies that, in point of spiritual perfection, she is above the Apostles.

2. St. Chrysostom, in his first passage, does not impute sin to her at all. He says God so disposed things for her as to shield her from the chance of sinning; that she was too admirable to be allowed to be betrayed by her best and purest feelings into sin. All that is implied in a spirit repugnant to a Catholic's reverence for her, is, that her woman's nature, viewed in itself and apart from the watchful providence of God's grace over her, would not have had strength to resist a hypothetical temptation,—a position which a Catholic will not care to affirm or deny, though he will feel great displeasure at having to discuss it at all. This too at least is distinctly brought out in the passage, viz., that in St. Chrysostom's mind, our Lady was not a mere physical instrument of the Incarnation, but that her soul, as well as her body, "ministered to the mystery," and needed to be duly prepared for it.

As to his second most extraordinary passage, I should not be candid, unless I simply admitted that it is as much at variance with what we hold, as it is solitary and singular in the writings of Antiquity. The Saint distinctly and (*pace illius*) needlessly, imputes to the Blessed Virgin, on the occasion in question, the sin or infirmity of vain-glory. He has a parallel passage in commenting on the miracle at the Marriage-feast. All that can be said to alleviate the startling character of these passages is, that it does not appear that St. Chrysostom would account such vain-glory in a woman any great sin.

3. Lastly, as to St. Cyril, I do not see that he declares that Mary actually doubted at the Crucifixion, but that, considering

she was a woman, it is likely she was tempted to doubt, and nearly doubted. Moreover, St. Cyril does not seem to consider such doubt, had it occurred, as any great sin.

Thus on the whole, all three Fathers, St. Basil and St. Cyril explicitly, and St. Chrysostom by implication, consider that on occasions she was, or might be, exposed to violent temptation to doubt; but two Fathers consider that she actually did sin, though she sinned lightly;—the sin being doubt, and on one occasion, according to St. Basil; and on two occasions, the sin being vain-glory, according to St. Chrysostom.

However, the strong language of these Fathers is not directed against our Lady's person, so much as against her nature. They seem to have participated with Ambrose, Jerome, and other Fathers in that low estimation of woman's nature which was general in their times. In the broad imperial world, the conception entertained of womankind was not high; it seemed only to perpetuate the poetical tradition of the "Varium et mutabile semper." Little was then known of that true nobility, which is exemplified in the females of the Gothic and German races, and in those of the old Jewish stock, Miriam, Deborah, Judith, Susanna, the forerunners of Mary. When then St. Chrysostom imputes vainglory to her, he is not imputing to her any thing worse than an infirmity, the infirmity of a nature, inferior to man's, and intrinsically feeble; as though the Almighty could have created a more excellent being than Mary, but could not have made a greater woman. Accordingly Chrysostom does not say that she sinned. He does not deny that she had all the perfections which woman could have; but he seems to have thought the capabilities of her nature were bounded, so that the utmost grace bestowed upon it could not raise it above that standard of perfection in which its elements resulted, and that to attempt more, would have been to injure, not benefit it. Of course I am not stating this as brought out in any part of his writings, but it seems to me to be the real sentiment of many of the ancients.

I will add that such a belief on the part of these Fathers, that the Blessed Virgin had committed a sin or a weakness, was not in itself inconsistent with the exercise of love and devotion to her (though I am not pretending that there is proof of its actual existence); and for this simple reason, that if sinlessness were a condition of inspiring devotion, we should not feel devotion to any but our Lady, not to St. Joseph, or to the Apostles, or to our Patron Saints.

Such then is the teaching of these three Fathers; now how far is it in antagonism to ours. On the one hand, we will not allow that our Blessed Lady ever sinned; we cannot bear the notion, entering, as we do, into the full spirit of St. Augustine's words, "Concerning the Holy Virgin Mary, I wish no question to be raised at all, when we are treating of sins." On the other hand, we admit, rather we maintain, that, except for the grace of God, she might have sinned; and that she may have been exposed to temptation in the sense in which our Lord was exposed to it, though as His Divine Nature made it impossible for Him to yield to it, so His grace preserved her from its assaults also. While then we do not hold that St. Simeon prophesied of temptation, when he said a sword would pierce her, still, if any one likes to say he did, we do not consider him heretical, provided he does not impute to her any sinful or inordinate emotion as the consequence to it. In this way St. Cyril may be let off altogether; and we have only to treat of the *paradoxa* or *anomala* of those great Saints, St. Basil and St. Chrysostom. I proceed to their controversial value.

II. I mean, that having determined what the Three Fathers say, and how far they are at issue with what Catholics hold now, I now come to the main question, viz. What is the authoritative force in controversy of what they thus say in opposition to Catholic teaching? I think I shall be able to show that it has no controversial force at all.

I begin by observing, that the main force of passages which can be brought from any Father or Fathers in controversy, lies in the fact that such passages represent the judgment or sentiment of their own respective countries; and again, I say that the force of that local judgment or sentiment lies in its being the existing expression of an Apostolical tradition. I am far, of course, from denying the claim of the teaching of a Father on our deference, arising out of his personal position and character;

or the claims of the mere sentiments of a Christian population on our careful attention, as a fact carrying with it, under circumstances, especial weight; but, in a question of doctrine, we must have recourse to the great source of doctrine, Apostolical Tradition, and a Father must represent his own people, and that people must be the witnesses of an uninterrupted Tradition from the Apostles, if any thing decisive is to come of any theological statement which is found in his writings; and if, in a particular case, there is no reason to suppose that he does echo the popular voice, or that that popular voice is transmitted from Apostolic times,—or (to take another channel of Tradition) unless the Father in question receives and reports his doctrine from the Bishops and Priests who instructed him on the very understanding and profession that it is Apostolical,—then, though it was not one Father but ten who said a thing, it would weigh nothing against the assertion of only one Father to the contrary, provided it was clear that that Father witnessed to an Apostolical Tradition. Now I do not say that I can decide the question by this issue with all the exactness which is conceivable, but still this is the issue by which it must be tried, and which I think will enable me to come to a satisfactory conclusion upon it.

Such, I say, being the issue, viz., that a doctrine reported by the Fathers, in order to have dogmatic force, must be a Tradition in its *source* or *form*, next, what is a Tradition, considered in its *matter?* It is a belief, which, be it *affirmative* or *negative*, is *positive*. The mere absence of a tradition in a country, is not a tradition the other way. If, for instance, there was no tradition in Syria and Asia Minor that the words "consubstantial with the Father," came from the Apostles, that would not be a tradition that they did not come from the Apostles, though of course it would be necessary for those who said that they did, to account for the ignorance of those countries as to the real fact.

The proposition "Christ is God," serves as an example of what I mean by an affirmative tradition; and "no one born of woman is born in God's favour," is an example of a negative tradition. Here it is observable that a tradition does not carry its own full explanation with it; it does but land (so to say) a proposition at the feet of the Apostles, and its interpretation has still to be determined,—as the Apostles' words in Scripture, however much theirs, need an interpretation. Thus I may accept the above negative Tradition, that "no one woman-born is born in God's favour," yet question its strict universality, as a point of criticism, saying that a general proposition admits of exceptions, that our Lord was born of woman, yet was the sinless and acceptable Priest and sacrifice for all men. So again the Arians allowed that "Christ was God," but they disputed about the meaning of the word "God."

Further, there are *explicit* traditions and *implicit*. By an explicit tradition I mean a doctrine which is conveyed in the letter of the proposition which has been handed down; and by implicit, one which lies in the force and virtue, not in the letter of the proposition. Thus it might be an Apostolical tradition that our Lord was the very Son of God, of one nature with the Father, and in all things equal to Him; and again a tradition that there was but one God: these would be explicit, but in them would necessarily be conveyed, moreover, the implicit tradition, that the Father and the Son were numerically one. Implicit traditions are positive traditions, as being strictly conveyed in positive.

Lastly, there are at least two ways of determining an Apostolical tradition:—1. When credible witnesses declare that it *is* Apostolical; as when three hundred Fathers at Nicæa stopped their ears at Arius's blasphemies; 2. When, in various places, independent witnesses enunciate one and the same doctrine, as St. Irenæus, St. Cyprian, and Eusebius assert, that the Apostles founded a Church, Catholic and One.

Now to apply these principles to the particular case, on account of which I have laid them down.

That "Mary is the new Eve," is a proposition answering to the *idea* of a Tradition. I am not prepared to say that it can be shown to have the first of the above two tests of its Apostolicity, viz., that the writers who record it, profess to have received it from the Apostles; but I conceive it has the second test, viz., that the writers are independent witnesses, as I have shown at length in the course of my Letter.

It is an explicit tradition; and by the force of it follow two others, which are implicit:—first (considering the condition of Eve in paradise), that Mary had no part in sin, and indefinitely large measures of grace; secondly (considering the doctrine of merits), that she has been exalted to glory proportionate to that grace.

This is what I have to observe on the argument in behalf of the Blessed Virgin. St. Justin, St. Irenæus, Tertullian, are witnesses of an Apostolical tradition, because in three distinct parts of the world they enunciate one and the same definite doctrine. And it is remarkable that they witness just for those three seats of Catholic teaching, where the truth in this matter was likely to be especially lodged. St. Justin speaks for Jerusalem, the see of St. James; St. Irenæus for Ephesus, the dwelling-place, the place of burial, of St. John; and Tertullian, who made a long residence at Rome, for the city of St. Peter and St. Paul.

Now, let us inquire, what can be produced on the other side, parallel to an argument like this? A tradition in its matter is a positive statement of belief; in its form it is a statement which comes from the Apostles: now, first, what statement of belief at all is witnessed to by St. Basil, St. Chrysostom, and St. Cyril? I cannot find any. They do but interpret certain passages in the Gospels to our Lady's disadvantage; is an interpretation a distinct statement of belief? but they do not all interpret the same passages. Nor do they agree together in their interpretation of those passages which one or other of them interprets so unsatisfactorily; for, while St. Chrysostom holds that our Lord spoke in correction of His mother at the wedding feast, St. Cyril on the contrary says that He wrought the miracle then, which He was Himself unwilling to work, in order to show "reverence to His Mother," and that she "having great authority for the working of the miracle, got the victory, persuading the Lord, as being her Son, as was fitting." But, taking only the statements which are in her disparagement, can we generalize them into one proposition? Shall we make it such as this, viz., "The Blessed Virgin during her earthly life committed actual sin?" If we mean by this, that there was a positive recognition of such a proposition in the country of St. Basil or St. Chrysostom, this surely is not to be gathered merely from their separate and independent comments on Scripture. All that can be gathered thence legitimately is, that, had there been a positive belief in her sinlessness in those countries, the Fathers in question would not have spoken of her in the terms which they have used; in other words, that there was no belief in her sinlessness then and there; but the absence of a belief is not a belief to the contrary, it is not that positive statement, which, as I have said, is required for the matter of a tradition.

Nor do the passages which I have quoted from these Fathers supply us with any tradition, viewed in its form, that is, as a statement which has come down from the Apostles. I have suggested two tests of such a statement:—one, when the writers who make it so declare that it was from the Apostles; and the other when, being independent of one another, they bear witness to one positive statement of doctrine. Neither test is fulfilled in this case. The three Fathers of the 4th and 5th centuries are but commenting on Scripture; and comments, though carrying with them of course, and betokening the tone of thought of the place and time to which they belong, are, *primâ facie* of a private and personal character. If they are more than this, the *onus probandi* lies with those who would have it so. Exegetical theology is one department of divine science, and dogmatic is another. On the other hand, the three Fathers of the 2nd century are all writing on dogmatic subjects, when they compare Mary to Eve.

Now to take the Three later Fathers one by one:—

1. As to St. Cyril, as I have said, he does not, strictly speaking, say more than that our Lady was grievously tempted. This does not imply sin, for our Lord was "tempted in all things like as we are, yet without sin." Moreover, it is this St. Cyril who spoke at Ephesus of the Blessed Virgin in terms of such high panegyric, as to make it more consistent in him to suppose that she was sinless, than that she was not.

2. St. Basil derived his notion, that the Blessed Virgin at the time of the Passion admitted a doubt about our Lord's mission, from Origen; and he, so far from professing to rest it

on Tradition, draws it as a theological conclusion from a received doctrine. Origen's characteristic fault was to prefer scientific reasonings to authority; and he exemplifies it in the case before us. In the middle age, the great obstacle to the reception of the doctrine of the Blessed Mary's immaculate conception, was the notion that, unless she had been in some sense a sinner, she could not have been redeemed. By an argument parallel to this, Origen argues, that since she was one of the redeemed, she must at one time or another have committed a sin. He says: "Are we to think, that the Apostles were scandalized, and not the Lord's Mother? If she suffered not scandal at our Lord's passion, then Jesus died not for her sins. If all have sinned and need the glory of God, being justified by His grace, and redeemed, certainly Mary at that time was scandalized." This is precisely the argument of Basil, as contained in the passage given above; his statement then of the Blessed Virgin's wavering in faith, instead of professing to be a tradition, carries with it an avowal of its being none at all.

However, I am not unwilling to grant that, whereas Scripture tells us that all were scandalized at our Lord's passion, there was some sort of traditional interpretation of Simeon's words, to the effect that she was in some sense included in that trial. How near the Apostolic era the tradition arose, cannot be determined; but this need not include the idea of sin in the Blessed Virgin, but only the presence of temptation and darkness of spirit. This tradition, whatever its authority, would be easily perverted, so as actually to impute sin to her, by such reasonings as that of Origen. Origen himself, in the passage I have quoted from him, refers to the sword of Simeon, and is the first to do so. St. Cyril, who, though an Alexandrian as well as Origen, represents a very different school of theology, has, as we have seen, the same interpretation for the piercing sword. It is also found in a Homily attributed to St. Amphilochius; and in that sixth Oration of Proclus, which, according to Tillemont and Ceillier, is not to be considered genuine. It is also found in a work incorrectly attributed to St. Augustine.

3. St. Chrysostom is, *par excellence*, the Commentator of the Church. As Commentator and Preacher, of all the Fathers, he

carries about him the most intense personality. In this lies his very charm, peculiar to himself. He is ever overflowing with thought, and he pours it forth with a natural engaging frankness, and an unwearied freshness and vigour. If he was in the practice of deeply studying and carefully criticizing what he delivered in public, he had in perfection the rare art of concealing his art. He ever speaks from himself, not of course without being impregnated with the fulness of a Catholic training, but still, not speaking by rule, but as if " trusting the lore of his own loyal heart." On the other hand, if it is not a paradox to say it, no one carries with him so little of the science, precision, consistency, gravity of a Doctor of the Church, as he who is one of the greatest. The difficulties are well known which he has occasioned to school theologians : his *obiter dicta* about our Lady are among them.

On the whole then I conclude that these three Fathers supply no evidence that, in what they say of her having failed in faith or humility on certain occasions mentioned in Scripture, they are reporting the decisions of Apostolical Tradition.

Such difficulties as the above are not uncommon in the writings of the Fathers. I will mention several :—

1. St. Gregory Nyssen is a great dogmatic divine; he too, like St. Basil, is of the school of Origen; and, in several passages of his works, he, like Origen, declares or suggests that future punishment will not be eternal. Those Anglicans who consider St. Chrysostom's passages in his Commentary on the Gospels to be a real argument against the Catholic belief of the Blessed Virgin's sinlessness, should explain why they do not feel St. Gregory Nyssen's teaching in his Catechetical Discourse, an argument against their own belief in the eternity of punishment.

2. Again, they believe in the proper divinity of our Lord, in spite of Bull's saying of the Ante-Nicene Fathers, "nearly all the ancient Catholics, who preceded Arius, have the appearance of being ignorant of the invisible and incomprehensible (*immensam*) nature of the Son of God;" an article of faith expressly contained in the Athanasian Creed, and enforced by its anathema.

3. The Divinity of the Holy Ghost is an integral part of the

fundamental doctrine of Christianity; yet St. Basil, in the fourth century, apprehending the storm of controversy which its assertion would raise, refrained from asserting it on an occasion when the Arians were on watch as to what he would say. And St. Athanasius took his part, on his keeping silence. Such inconsistencies take place continually, and no Catholic doctrine but suffers from them at times, until what has been preserved by Tradition is formally pronounced to be apostolical by definition of the Church.

Before concluding, I shall briefly take notice of two questions which may be asked me.

1. How are we to account for the absence, at Antioch or Cæsarea, of a tradition of our Lady's sinlessness? I consider that it was obliterated or confused by the Arian troubles in the countries in which those Sees are included.

It is not surely wonderful, if, in Syria and Asia Minor, the seat in the fourth century of Arianism and Semi-arianism, the prerogatives of the mother were obscured together with the essential glory of the Son, or if they who denied the tradition of His divinity, forgot the tradition of her sinlessness. Christians in those countries and times, however religious themselves, however orthodox their teachers, were necessarily under peculiar disadvantages.

Now let it be observed that Basil grew up in the very midst of Semi-arianism, and had direct relations with that portion of its professors who had been reconciled to the Church and accepted the Homoüsion. It is not wonderful then, if he had no firm habitual hold upon a doctrine which (though Apostolical) was in his day so much in the background as yet all over Christendom, as our Lady's sinlessness.

As to Chrysostom, not only was he in close relations with the once Semi-arian Cathedra of Antioch, to the disavowal of the rival succession there, recognized by Rome and Alexandria, but, as his writings otherwise show, he came under the teaching of the celebrated Antiochene School, celebrated, that is, at once for its Scripture criticism, and (orthodox as it was itself) for the successive outbreaks of heresy among its members. These outbreaks began in Paul of Samosata, were continued in the Semi-arian pupils of Lucian, and ended in Nestorius. The famous Theodore, and Diodorus, of the same school, who, though not heretics themselves, have a bad name in the Church, were, Diodorus the master, and Theodore the fellow-pupil, of St. Chrysostom. (Vid. *Arians of the Fourth Cent.*, p. 8, and *Doctr. Devel.* p. 252.) Here then is a natural explanation, why St. Chrysostom, even more than St. Basil, should be wanting in a clear perception of the place of the Blessed Virgin in the Evangelical Dispensation.

2. How are we to account for the passages in the Gospels, which are the occasion of the Fathers' remarks to her disparagement? They seem to me intended to discriminate between our Lord's work who is our Teacher and Redeemer, and the ministrative office of His Mother.

As to the words of Simeon, as interpreted by St. Basil and St. Cyril, there is nothing in the sacred text which obliges us to consider the "sword" to mean doubt rather than anguish; but Matth. xii. 46—50, with its parallels Mark iii. 31—35, and Luke viii. 19—21; Luke xi. 27, 28, and John ii. 4, require some explanation.

I observe then, that, when our Lord commenced His ministry, and during it, as one of His chief self-sacrifices, He separated Himself from all ties of earth, in order to fulfil the typical idea of a teacher and priest; and to give an example to His priests after Him; and especially to manifest by this action the cardinal truth, as expressed by the Prophet, "I am, I am the Lord, and there is no Saviour besides Me." As to His Priests, they, after Him, were to be of the order of that Melchizedech, who was "without father and without mother;" for "no man, being a soldier to God, entangleth himself with secular business:" and "no man putting his hand to the plough, and looking back, is fit for the kingdom of God." As to the Levites, who were His types in the Old Law, there was that honourable history of their zeal for God, when they even slew their own brethren and companions who had committed idolatry; "who said to his father and to his mother, I do not know you, and to his brethren, I know you not, and their own children they have not known." To this separation even from His Mother He refers

K

by anticipation at twelve years old in His words, "How is it that you sought Me? Did you not know that I must be about My Father's business?"

This separation from her, with whom He had lived thirty years and more, was not to last beyond the time of His ministry. She seems to have been surprised when she first heard of it, for St. Luke says, on occasion of His staying in the Temple, "they understood not the word, that He spoke to them." Nay, she seems hardly to have understood it at the marriage-feast; but He, in dwelling on it more distinctly then, implied also that it was not to last long. He said, "Woman, what have I to do with thee? My hour is not yet come,"—the hour of His triumph, when His Mother was to take her predestined place in His kingdom. In saying the hour was not yet come, He implied that the hour would come, when He would have to do with her, and she might ask and obtain from Him miracles. Accordingly, St. Augustine thinks that that hour had come, when on the Cross He said, "*Consummatum est*," and, after this ceremonial estrangement of some years, He recognized His mother and committed her to the beloved disciple. Thus by marking out the beginning and the end of the period of exception, when she could not exert her influence upon Him, He signifies more clearly, by the contrast, that her presence with Him, and her power, was to be the rule. In a higher sense than He spoke to the Apostles, He seems to address her in the words, "Because I have spoken these things, sorrow hath filled your heart. But I will see you again, and your heart shall rejoice, and your joy no man shall take from you." (*Vid. Sermon* iii. *in Sermons on Subjects of the Day, on " Our Lord's Last Supper and His First.*")

P.S. Third Edition: On the comment of St. Irenæus, &c., upon our Lord's words to the Blessed Virgin at the marriage-feast, vid. my note on Athanas. Orat. iii. 41.

Also, I might have added to the present Note the passage in Tertullian, Carn. Christ. § 7, as illustrating, by its contrast with § 17 (quoted above, p. 36), the distinction between doctrinal tradition and personal opinion, could I have considered it clear that he included the Blessed Virgin in the unbelief which he imputes to our Lord's brethren; for he expressly separates her off from them. The passage runs thus on the text, "Who is My Mother? and who are My Brethren?"

"The Lord's brothers had not believed in Him, as is contained in the Gospel published before Marcion. His Mother, equally, *is not described* (non demonstratur) *to have adhered to Him*, whereas Martha and Mary were frequent in His intercourse. In this place at length their (eorum) incredulity is evident; while He was teaching the way of life, was preaching the kingdom of God, was working for the cure of ailments and diseases, though strangers were riveted to Him, these, so much the nearest to Him (tam proximi), were away. At length they come upon Him, and stand without, nor enter, not reckoning forsooth on what was going on within. Nor even do they wait; as if they were bringing thither something necessary, which He then was especially employed on; but they go on to interrupt, and wish Him recalled from so great a work."

## NOTE D. PAGE 96.

Canisius, in his work *de Mariá Deipará Virgine*, p. 514, while engaged in showing the carefulness with which the Church distinguishes the worship of God from the *cultus* of the Blessed Virgin, observes, "Lest the Church should depart from *Latria* (i. e. the worship of God) she has instituted the public supplications in the Liturgy in perpetuity in such wise as to address them directly to God the Father, and not to the Saints, according to that common form of praying, 'Almighty, everlasting God,' &c.; and the said prayers which they also call 'Collects,' she generally ends in this way, 'through Jesus Christ, Thy Son, our Lord.'" He says more to the same purpose, but the two points here laid down are sufficient; viz. that as to the Latin Missal, Ritual, and Breviary, 1. Saints are not directly addressed in these books: and 2. prayers end with the name of Jesus. An apposite illustration of both of these, that is, in what is omitted and what is introduced, is supplied by the concluding prayer of the Offertory in the Latin Mass. If in any case the name of 'our Lady and all Saints' may be substituted at the end of a prayer for our Lord's name, it would be when the object addressed is, not God the Father, but the Son, or the Holy Trinity; but let us observe how the prayer in question runs:—

"Suscipe, Sancta Trinitas" — "Receive, *O Holy Trinity*, this oblation which we make to Thee, in memory of the Passion, Resurrection, and Ascension of our Lord Jesus Christ, and *in honour of* the Blessed Mary, Ever-Virgin, of Blessed John Baptist, and of the Holy Apostles Peter and Paul, and of these and all Saints, that it may avail for their honour and our salvation, and that they may vouchsafe to intercede for us in heaven, whose memory we celebrate on earth, *Through the same Christ our Lord*. Amen."

When in occasional Collects the intercession of the Blessed Mary is introduced, it does not supersede mention of our Lord as the Intercessor. Thus in the Post-communion on the Feast of the Circumcision,—

"May this communion, O Lord, purify us from guilt; and at the intercession of Blessed Virgin Mary, Mother of God, make us partakers of the heavenly remedy, through the same Lord Jesus Christ. Amen."

In like manner, when the Son is addressed, and the intercession of Mary and the Saints is supplicated, His own merits are introduced at the close, as on the Feast of the Seven Dolours:—

"God, at whose passion, according to the prophecy of Simeon, the most sweet soul of the glorious Virgin-Mother Mary was pierced through with the sword of sorrow, mercifully grant, that we, who reverently commemorate her piercing and passion, may, by the intercession of the glorious merits and prayers of the Saints who faithfully stood by the Cross, *obtain the happy fruit of Thy Passion,* who livest and reignest, &c."

"We offer to Thee, Lord Jesus Christ, our prayers and sacrifices, humbly supplicating, that we, who renew in our prayers the piercing of the most sweet soul of Thy Blessed Mother Mary, by the manifold compassionate intervention of both her and her holy companions under the Cross, *by the merits of Thy death,* may merit a place with the Blessed, who livest, &c."

Now let us observe how far less observant of dogmatic exactness, how free and fearless, is the formal Greek devotion:—

1. "We have risen from sleep, and we fall down before Thee, O good God; and we sing to Thee the Angelic Hymn, O powerful God. Holy, holy, holy art Thou, God; have mercy on us through the Theotocos.

"Thou hast raised me from my bed and slumber, O God. Lighten my mind, and open my heart and lips, to sing of Thee, Holy Trinity. Holy, holy, holy art Thou, God; have mercy on us through the Theotocos.

"Soon will come the Judge, and the deeds of all will be laid bare . . . Holy, holy, holy art Thou, God; have mercy on us through the Theotocos."—*Horologium,* p. 2, *Venet.* 1836: vide also, pp. 34. 48. 52. Also, *Eucholog. Venet.* p. 358.

2. "O God, who lookest on the earth, and makest it tremble, deliver us from the fearful threatenings of earthquake, Christ our God; and send down on us Thy rich mercies, and save us, at the intercessions (πρεσβείαις) of the Theotocos."—*Ibid.* p. 224. Vid. also *Pentecostar.* p. 14.

3. "O Holy God, . . . visit us in Thy goodness, pardon us every sin, sanctify our souls, and grant us to serve Thee in holiness all the days of our life, at the intercessions (πρεσβείαις) of the Holy Theotocos and all the Saints, &c."—*Euchologium*, p. 64. *Venet.* 1832.

4. "Again, and still again, let us beseech the Lord in peace. Help, save, pity, preserve us, O God [through] her, the all-holy, Immaculate, most Blessed, and glorious, (διαφύλαξον ἡμᾶς ὁ Θεὸς, τῆς παναγίας,) &c."—*Euchologium*, p. 92. *Venet.* 1832. Vid. also *Pentecostar.* p. 232; and *passim*.

5. "Lord, Almighty Sovereign, . . . restore and raise from her bed this Thy servant, &c. . . . at the intercession (πρεσβείαις) of the all-undefiled Theotocos and all the Saints."—*Ibid.* p. 142.

6. "Have mercy and pardon, (for Thou alone hast power to remit sins and iniquities,) at the intercession of Thy all-holy Mother and all the Saints."—*Ibid.* p. 150.

7. "O Lord God Almighty, . . . bless and hallow Thy place . . . at the intercession (πρεσβείαις) of our glorious Lady, Mary, Mother of God and Ever-Virgin."—*Eucholog.* p. 389.

Is the Blessed Virgin ever called "our Lady," as here, in the Latin Prayers? whereas it is a frequent title of her in the Greek.

8. "Save me, my God, from all injury and harm, Thou who art glorified in Three Persons . . . and guard Thy flock at the intercessions (ἐντεύξεσιν) of the Theotocos."—*Pentecostarium*, p. 59. *Venet.* 1820. Vid. also Goar, *Eucholog.* p. 30.

9. "In the porch of Solomon there lay a multitude of sick . . . Lord, send to us Thy great mercies at the intercession (πρεσβείαις) of the Theotocos."—*Pentecostar.* p. 84. Vid. also Goar, *Eucholog.* pp. 488. 543.

10. "O great God, the Highest, who alone hast immortality . . . prosper our prayer as the incense before Thee . . . that we may remember even in the night Thy holy Name, . . . and

rise anew in gladness of soul . . . bringing our prayers and supplications to Thy loving-kindness in behalf of our own sins and of all Thy people, whom visit in mercy at the intercessions (πρεσβείαις) of the Holy Theotocos."—*Ibid.* p. 232. Vid. *Horolog.* p. 192. *Venet.* 1836.

11. Between the Trisagion and Epistle in Mass. "O Holy God, who dwellest in the holy place, whom with the voice of their Trisagion the Seraphim do praise, &c. . . . sanctify our souls and bodies, and grant us to serve Thee in holiness all the days of our life, at the intercession (πρεσβείαις) of the Holy Theotocos and all the Saints."—*Eucholog.* p. 64. *Venet.* 1832.

12. In the early part of Mass. "Lift up the horn of Christians, and send down on us Thy rich mercies, by the power of the precious and life-giving Cross, by the grace of Thy light-bringing, third-day resurrection from the dead, at the intercession (πρεσβείαις) of our All-holy Blessed Lady Mary, Mother of God and Ever-Virgin, and all Thy Saints."—Assemani, *Codex Liturg.* t. v. p. 71. *Rite of St. James.*

13. At the Offertory at Mass. "In honour and memory of our singularly blessed and glorious Queen, Mary Theotocos and Ever-Virgin; at whose intercession, O Lord, receive, O Lord, this sacrifice unto Thy altar which is beyond the heavens."—Goar, *Euchol.* p. 58. *Rite of St. Chrysostom.*

14. In the Commemoration at Mass. "*Cantors.* Hail, Mary, full of grace, &c. &c. . . . for thou hast borne the Saviour of our souls. *Priest.* [Remember, Lord] especially the most Holy Immaculate, &c. . . . Mary. *Cantors.* It is meet truly to bless (μακαρίζειν) thee, the Theotocos . . . more honourable than the Cherubim, &c. . . . thee we magnify, who art truly the Theotocos. O Full of Grace, in thee the whole creation rejoices, the congregation of Angels, and the race of men, O sanctified shrine, and spiritual Paradise, boast of virgins," &c.—Assemani, t. v. p. 44. *Jerusalem Rite.*

15. In the Commemoration at Mass. "*Priest.* Especially and first of all, we make mention of the Holy, glorious, and Ever-Virgin Mary, &c. *Deacon.* Remember her, Lord God, and at her holy and pure prayers be propitious, have mercy upon us, and favourably hear us. *Priest.* Mother of our Lord Jesus Christ, pray for me to thy Son Only-begotten, who came

of thee, that, having remitted my sins and debts, He may accept from my humble and sinful hands this sacrifice, which is offered by my vileness on this altar, through thy intercession, Mother most holy."—*Ibid.* p. 186. *Syrian Rite.*

16. Apparently, after the Consecration. "*The Priest incenses thrice before the Image* (*imagine*) *of the Virgin, and says:* Rejoice, Mary, beautiful dove, who hast borne for us God, the Word; thee we salute with the Angel Gabriel, saying, Hail, full of grace, the Lord is with thee, Hail, Virgin, true Queen; hail, glory of our race, thou hast borne Emmanuel. We ask, remember us, O faithful advocate, in the sight of our Lord Jesus Christ, that He put away from us our sins."— *Ibid.* t. vii., *pars* 2*da. in fin.* p. 20. *Alexandrian Rite.*

17. At the Communion in Mass. "Forgive, our God, remit, pardon me my trespasses as many as I have committed, whether in knowledge or in ignorance, whether in word or in deed. All these things pardon me, as Thou art good and kind to men, at the intercession (πρεσβείαις) of Thy all-undefiled and Ever-Virgin Mother. Preserve me uncondemned, that I may receive Thy precious and undefiled Body, for the healing of my body and soul."—Goar, *Euchologium,* p. 66.

18. After Communion at Mass. "O Lord, be merciful to us, bless us, let Thy countenance be seen upon us, and pity us. Lord, save Thy people, bless Thine heritage, &c., . . . through the prayers and addresses (orationes) which the Lady of us all, Mother of God, the divine (diva) and Holy Mary, and the four bright holy ones, Michael," &c., &c.—Renaudot, *Liturg. Orient.* t. i. p. 29. *Coptic Rite of St. Basil.* Vid. also *ibid.* pp. 29. 37. 89. 515, *of St. Basil, Coptic, of St. Gregory, Coptic, of Alexandria, Greek, and of Ethiopia.*

19. After Communion at Mass. "We have consummated this holy service (λειτουργίαν), as we have been ordered, O Lord . . . we, sinners, and Thine unworthy servants, who have been made worthy to serve at Thy holy altar, in offering to Thee the bloodless sacrifice, the immaculate Body and the precious Blood of the Great God, our Saviour, Jesus Christ, to Thy glory, the unoriginate Father, and the glory of Him, Thy only-begotten Son, and of the Holy Ghost, good, life-giving, and consubstantial with Thee. We ask a place on Thy right

hand in Thy fearful and just day through the intercession (διὰ τῶν πρεσβειῶν) and prayers of our most glorious Lady, Mary, Mother of God, and Ever-Virgin, and of all saints."—Assemani, *Cod. Liturg.* t. vii. p. 85. *Rite of Alexandria.*

20. After Communion at Mass. " We thank Thee, Lord, Lover of men, Benefactor of our souls, that also on this day Thou hast vouchsafed us Thy heavenly and immortal mysteries. Direct our way aright, confirm us all in Thy fear, &c., . . . at the prayers and supplications of the glorious Theotocos and Ever-Virgin Mary, and of all Thy saints."—*Euchol̥og.* p. 86. *Venet.* 1832.

21. Concluding words of Mass. "Blessed is He who has given us His holy Body and precious Blood. We have received grace and found life, by virtue of the Cross of Jesus Christ. To Thee, O Lord, we give thanks, &c. Praise to Mary, who is the glory of us all, who has brought forth for us the Eucharist."—Renaudot, *Liturg. Orient.* t. i. p. 522. *Rite of Ethiopia.*

I will add some of the instances, which have caught my eye in these ecclesiastical books, of expressions about the Blessed Virgin, which, among Latins, though occurring in some Antiphons, belong more to the popular than to the formal and appointed devotions paid to the Blessed Virgin.

22. " Thee we have as a tower and a harbour, and an acceptable ambassadress (πρέσβιν) to the God whom thou didst bear, Mother of God who hadst no spouse, the salvation of believers."—*Pentecostar.* p. 209. *Venet.* 1820.

23. " O Virgin alone holy and undefiled, who hast miraculously (ἀσπόρως) conceived God, intercede (πρέσβευε) for the salvation of the soul of thy servant."—*Euchol̥og.* p. 439. *Venet.* 1832.

24. " Show forth thy speedy protection and aid and mercy on thy servant, and still the waves, thou pure one, of vain thoughts, and raise up my fallen soul, O Mother of God. For I know, O Virgin, I know that thou hast power for whatever thou willest."—*Ibid.* p. 679.

25. " Joachim and Anna were set free from the reproach of childlessness, and Adam and Eve from the corruption of death,

O undefiled, in thy holy birth. And thy people keeps festival upon it, being ransomed from the guilt of their offences in crying to thee. The barren bears the Theotocos, and the nurse of Life."—*Horolog.* p. 198. *Venet.* 1836.

26. " Let us now run earnestly to the Theotocos, sinners as we are, and low, and let us fall in repentance, crying from the depth of our souls, Lady, aid us, taking compassion on us. Make haste, we perish under the multitude of our offences. Turn us not, thy servants, empty away; for we have thee as our only hope."—*Ibid.* p. 470. Vid. "My whole hope I repose in thee."—*Triodion*, p. 94. *Venet.* 1820.

27. " We have gained thee for a wall of refuge, and the all-perfect salvation of souls, and a release (πλατυσμὸν) in afflictions, and in thy light we ever rejoice; O Queen, even now through suffering and danger preserve us."—*Ibid.* p. 474.

28. "By thy mediation, Virgin, I am saved."—*Triod.* p. 6. *Venet.* 1820.

29. "The relief of the afflicted, the release of the sick, O Virgin Theotocos, save this city and people; the peace of those who are oppressed by war, the calm of the tempest-tost, the sole protection of the faithful."—Goar, *Eucholog.* p. 478.

30. All through the Office Books are found a great number of Collects and Prayers to the Blessed Virgin, called Theotocia, whereas in the Latin Offices addresses to her scarcely get beyond the Antiphons. There are above 100 of them in the Euchology, above 170 in the Pentecostarium, close upon 350 in the Triodion. These, according to Renaudot, are sometimes collected together into separate volumes. (*Liturg. Orient.* t. ii, p. 98.)

31. At p. 424 of the *Horologium* there is a collection of 100 invocations in her honour, arranged for the year.

32. At p. 271 of the *Euchologium*, is a form of prayer to her "in the confession of a sinner," consisting of thirty-six collects, concluding with a Gospel, supplication, &c. If there were any doubt of the difference which the Greeks make between her and the Saints, one of these would be evidence of it. "*Take with you* (παράλαβε) the multitude of Archangels and of

the heavenly hosts, and the Forerunner, &c., . . . and make intercession (πρεσβείαν), Holy One, in my behalf with God," p. 275. Vid. also *ibid.* p. 390, &c.

33. There is another form of prayer to her at p. 640, of forty-three collects or verses, "in expectation of war," arranged to form an Iambic acrostic, "O undefiled, be the ally of my household." Among other phrases we read here, "Thou art the head commander (ὁ ἀρχιστράτηγος) of Christians;" . . . "They in their chariots and horses, we, thy people, in thy name;" "with thy spiritual hand cast down the enemies of thy people;" "Thy power runs with thy will (σύνδρομον ἔχεις), &c." "Deliver not thine heritage, O holy one, into the hands of the heathen, lest they shall say, where is the Mother of God in whom they trusted?" "Hear from thy holy Temple, thy servants, O pure one, and pour out God's wrath upon the Gentiles that do not know thee, and the kingdoms that have not faithfully called upon thy celebrated name."

34. It is remarkable, that, not only the Jacobites, but even the Nestorians agree with the Orthodox in the unlimited honours they pay to the Theotocos. "No one," says Renaudot, "has accused the Orientals of deficiency in the legitimate honours, which are the right of the Deipara; but many have charged them with having sometimes been extravagant in that devotion, and running into superstition, which accusation is not without foundation."—t. i. p. 257.

Another remark of his is in point here. The extracts above made are in great measure from Greek service-books of this day; but even those which are not such are evidence according to their date and place of opinions and practices, then and there existing. "Their weight does not depend on the authority of the writers, but on the use of the Churches. Those prayers had their authors, who indeed were not known; but, when once it was clear that they had been used in Mass, who their authors were ceased to be a question."—t. i. p. 173. The existing manuscripts can hardly be supposed to be mere compositions, but are records of rites.

I say then, first:—That usage, which, after a split has taken place in a religious communion, is found to obtain equally in each of its separated parts, may fairly be said to have existed before the split occurred. The concurrence of Orthodox, Nestorian, and Jacobite in the honours they pay to the Blessed Virgin, is an evidence that those honours were paid to her in their " Undivided Church."

Next:—Passages such as the above, taken from the formal ritual of the Greeks, are more compromising to those who propose entering into communion with them, than such parallel statements as occur in unauthoritative devotions of the Latins.

## NOTE E. PAGE 113.

I find the following very apposite passage at note t, p. 390, of Vol. I. of Mr. Morris's "Jesus the Son of Mary," a work full of learning, which unhappily I forgot to consult, till my Letter was finished and in type.

"An error of this sort [that our Lady is in the Holy Eucharist] was held by some persons, and is condemned in the following language by Benedict XIV.[?], as has been pointed out to me by my old and valued friend, Father Faber: 'This doctrine was held to be erroneous, dangerous, and scandalous, and the *cultus* was reprobated, which in consequence of it, they asserted was to be paid to the most Blessed Virgin in the Sacrament of the Altar.'"

. *Lambertini de Canonizatione Sanctorum.* Lib. iv. p. 2, c. 31, n. 32.

De cultu erga Deiparam in Sacramento Altaris.

Non multis abhinc annis prodiit *Liber de cultu erga Deiparam in Sacramento altaris*, auctore Patre Zephyrino de Someire Recollecto Sancti Francisci, in quo asserebatur, in Sacramento altaris aliquam illius partem adesse, eandem videlicet carnem, quam olim ejus sanctissima anima vivificavit, eumdemque illum sanguinem, qui in ejus venis continebatur, et ipsum lac, quo ejus ubera plena erant. Addebatur, nos habere in Sacramento non tantum sanguinem Deiparæ, quatenus in carnem et ossa Christi mutatus est, sed etiam partem sanguinis in propria specie; neque solum veram carnem ipsius, sed etiam aliquid singulorum membrorum, quia sanguis, et lac, ex quibus formatum et nutritum fuit corpus Christi, missa fuerunt ab omnibus et singulis membris Beatissimæ Virginis.

Etiam Christophorus de Vega in volumine satis amplo, quod inscribitur, *THEOLOGIA MARIANA* Lugduni edito ann. 1653, fusius ea omnia prosecutus est: sed Theophilus Raynaudus in suis *Diptychis Marianis* t. 7. p. 65, ca reprobat, asseritque hæresim sapere juxta Guidonem Carmelitam *in Summa de hæresibus tract. de hæresi Græcorum* c. 13., cujus verba sunt hæc : " *Tertius decimus error Græcorum est. Dicunt enim, quod reliquiæ Panis consecrati sunt reliquiæ corporis Beatæ Virginis. Hic error stultitiæ et amentiæ plenus est. Nam corpus Christi sub qualilibet parte hostiæ consecratæ integrum manet. Itaque quælibet pars, a tota consecrata hostia divisa et separata, est verum corpus Christi. Hæreticum autem est et fatuum dicere, quod corpus Christi sit corpus Virginis matris suæ, sicut hæreticum esset dicere, quod Christus esset Beata Virgo ; quia distinctorum hominum distincta sunt corpora, nec tantus honor debetur corpori virginis, quantus debetur corpori Christi, cui ratione Divini Suppositi debetur honor latriæ, non corpori Virginis. Igitur dicere, reliquias hostiæ consecratæ esse reliquias corporis Beatæ Virginis est hæreticum manifeste.*"

Porro Theologorum Princeps D. Thomas 3 *part. quæst.* 31, *art.* 5, docet primo, Christi corpus conceptum fuisse ex Beatæ Virginis castissimis et purissimis sanguinibus non quibuscunque, sed "*perductis ad quamdam ampliorem digestionem per virtutem generativam ipsius, ut essent materia apta ad conceptum,*" cum Christi conceptio fuerit secundum conditionem naturæ ; materiamque aptam, sive purissimum sanguinem in conceptione Christi sola Spiritus Sancti operatione in utero Virginis adunatam, et in prolem formatum fuisse ; ita ut vere dicatur corpus Christi ex purissimis et castissimis sanguinibus Beatæ Virginis fuisse formatum. Docet secundo, non potuisse corpus Christi formari de aliqua substantia, videlicet de carne et ossibus Beatissimæ Virginis, cum sint partes integrantes corpus ipsius ; ideoque subtrahi non potuissent sine corruptione, et ejus diminutione : illud vero, quod aliquando dicitur, Christum de Beata Virgine carnem sumpsisse, intelligendum esse et explicandum, non quod materia corporis ejus fuerit actu caro, sed sanguis qui est potentia caro. Docet demum tertio, quomodo subtrahi potuerit ex corpore Adam aliqua ejus pars absque ipsius diminutione, cum Adam institutus ut principium quoddam humanæ naturæ, aliquid habuerit ultra partes sui corporis personales, quod ab eo subtractum est pro formanda Heva, salva ipsius integritate in ratione perfecti corporis humani: quæ locum habere non potuerunt in Beatissima Virgine, quæ uti singulare individuum habuit perfectissimum corpus humanum, et aptissimam materiem ad Christi corpus formandum, quantum est ex parte feminæ, et ad ejus naturalem generationem. Ex quo fit, ut non potuerit, salva integritate Beatæ Virginis, aliquid subtrahi, quod dici posset de substantia corporis ipsius.

Itaque, cum per hanc doctrinam, Fidei principiis conjunctissimam, directe et expressis verbis improbata remanserint asserta in citato libro Patris Zephyrini, ejus doctrina habita est tanquam "*erronea, periculosa, et scandalosa,*" reprobatusque fuit cultus, quem ex ea præstandum Beatissimæ Virgini in Sacramento altaris asserebat. Loquendi autem formulæ a nonnullis Patribus adhibitæ, *Caro Mariæ est caro Christi Etc.* *Nobis carnem Mariæ manducandum ad salutem dedit,* ita explicandæ sunt, non ut dicamus, in Christo aliquid esse, quod sit Mariæ; sed Christum conceptum esse ex Maria Virgine, materiam ipsa ministrante in similitudinem naturæ et speciei, et ideo filium ejus esse. Sic, quia caro Christi fuit sumpta de David, ut expresse dicitur *ad Romanos* 1. "*Qui factus est ex semine David secundum carnem,*" David dicitur Christus, ut notat S. Augustinus *enarrat. in Psalm.* 144, *num.* 2. "*Intelligitur laus ipsi David, laus ipsi Christo. Christus autem secundum carnem David, quia Filius David.*" Et infra: "*Quia itaque ex ipso Christus secundum carnem, ideo David.*" Est item solemnis Scripturæ usus, loquendo de parentibus, ut caro unius vocitetur caro alterius. Sic Laban *Gen.* 29 dixit Jacob.: "*Os meum es, et caro mea;*" et Judas, loquendo de fratre suo Joseph, *Gen.* 27. ait: "*Frater enim, et caro nostra est:*" et *Lev.* 18 legitur: "*Soror patris tui caro est patris tui, et soror matris tuæ caro est matris tuæ;*" absque eo quod hinc inferri possit, ut in Jacob fuerit aliqua actualis pars corporis Laban, aut in Joseph pars Judæ, aut in filio pars aliqua patris. Igitur id solum affirmare licet, in Sacramento esse carnem Christi assumptam ex Maria, ut ait Sanctus Ambrosius relatus in canone *Omnia, de Consecrat. distinct.* 2 his verbis: "*Hæc caro mea est pro mundi vita, et, ut mirabilius loquar, non alia plane, quam quæ nata est de Maria, et passa in cruce, et resurrexit de sepulcro; hæc, inquam, ipsa est.*" Et infra loquens de corpore Christi: "*Illud vere, illud sane, quod sumptum est de Virgine, quod passum est, et sepultum.*"

P.S. Second Edition: A correspondent of the Weekly Register has pointed out that Oswald's work (vid. supr. p. 103) is on the Index. Vide page 5 of "Appendix Librorum Prohibitorum a die 6 Septembris, 1852, ad mensem junium, 1858."

THE END.

www.ingramcontent.com/pod-product-compliance
Lightning Source LLC
Chambersburg PA
CBHW030254170426
43202CB00009B/738